UNIVERSITY OF NORTH CAROLINA
STUDIES IN THE ROMANCE LANGUAGES AND LITERATURES
Number 44

STUDIES
IN ROMANCE PHILOLOGY AND LITERATURE

STUDIES IN ROMANCE
PHILOLOGY AND
LITERATURE

BY

MARIO A. PEI

CHAPEL HILL
THE UNIVERSITY OF NORTH CAROLINA PRESS

Copyright, 1966, by
The University of North Carolina Press

Reprinted 1966

by Permission

of the Original Publisher

GARRETT PUBLISHING COMPANY
103 West 49th Street
New York, N.Y. 10019

Hans Namuth, New York 19

Mario A. Pei

CONTENTS

		Pages
	Foreword	9
	Mario Pei	11
	TABULA GRATULATORIA	15
I	OLD FRENCH DEMONSTRATIVES	17
II	FRENCH 'ICIL'	22
III	ACCUSATIVE OR OBLIQUE	24
IV	ACCUSATIVE versus OBLIQUE IN PORTUGUESE	55
V	«IN CASA I FRESCOBALDI»	58
VI	FRENCH -ier FROM LATIN -ariu	63
VII	LATIN AND ITALIAN FRONT VOWELS	79
VIII	INTERVOCALIC OCCLUSIVES IN EAST AND WEST ROMANCE	85
IX	AN IMMORTAL CHARACTER IN FRENCH LITERATURE	100
X	ETRUSCAN AND INDO-EUROPEAN CASE ENDINGS	108
XI	REFLECTIONS ON THE ORIGIN OF THE ROMANCE LANGUAGES	114
XII	*Ab* AND THE SURVIVAL OF THE LATIN GENITIVE IN ITALIAN	120
XIII	A NEW METHODOLOGY FOR ROMANCE CLASSIFICATION	123

FOREWORD

Our twentieth century will undoubtedly be characterized as one of the most practical-minded ages of all times, though there is a measure of poetry in our trying to communicate with the outer reaches of space to ascertain whether there are any rational beings with whom we can exchange philosophies. Or it may also turn out that it will be called the Age of Dynamism. In retrospect, however, some historians may find it difficult to distinguish between some of our dynamism and Saint Vitus' dance.

A certain lack of perspective is already evident in our time regarding some academic disciplines. This is true not only of the layman, but also of the practitioners of these same disciplines. It would seem that there are fashions in the relative importance of academic subjects just as fickle as in our workaday world. If this be true, why should anyone in his right mind be so benighted as to choose Romance Philology as a lifelong career? Even a cursory investigation should convince the most starry-eyed novice that this subject requires as much preparation as many other much more materially rewarding and glamorous professions. When to this arduous, exacting and time-consuming preparation is added the further uncertainty of gaining a livelihood, as well as the dismaying spectacle of embarrassing and needless interdisciplinary bickering, it is small wonder that there are today so very few Romance Philologists. Today's practical student would have to be a poet indeed to make such a foolhardy choice. Yet it appears that there are still a few of these courageous souls around. May their tribe increase!

As if all this sad state of affairs were not enough to discourage the bold, the lack of introductory textbooks in English should frighten even the most daring.

There is yet another obstacle strewn across the path of anyone who would aspire to become a Romance Philologist in our practical age. Aside from its intrinsic difficulties, some members of related disciplines who are but able to mention the field deprecatingly, will unhesitatingly imply that it is as useless as chess. Or at best, that it is a luxury that one has to be able to afford. Such statements make one wonder whether we have not lost sight of the forest because of the trees. It should be obvious that the primary purpose of linguistics is to try to determine the nature of language. By extension, this research contributes to a better understanding of man and the universe. Romance Philology has greatly contributed and should continue to contribute to this worthy goal. Because of its unique recorded history, it serves as a check to many unbridled flights of fancy. For that reason alone it is worth its weight in any coin of the realm.

In view of the above statements, it seems superfluous to add that it is of paramount importance to do our very best to make linguistics and philology of any persuasion more widely known, among students and laymen alike. For this purpose we need many mansions in our house. We also need those who know how to make the necessary fundamentals accessible to anyone interested in our respective specialties. Unfortunately, we have very few *vulgarisateurs* who have both enough knowledge and the flair for the picturesque to arouse interest where it may do us all some good. One of the very few who has had the temerity to attempt proselytizing for the common weal is Mario Pei. May his tribe increase!

FAIRLEIGH DICKINSON UNIVERSITY   JOHN FISHER

MARIO PEI

Born in Rome, Italy, on February 16, 1901, Mario Pei had already had two years of schooling in his native city when he came to the United States in 1908. His elementary education was continued in various New York City public schools and completed in the parochial school of St. John Evangelist. It was here that he won his earliest academic laurels in 1914: the first gold medal in the Mooney contest for English composition among all the parochial schools of Greater New York, and a four-year scholarship to St. Francis Xavier High School. In this institution, where four years of Latin, three and a half of Greek, and three of a modern language were required subjects, he spent the next four years, carrying off every class prize in languages, mathematics and the sciences. At seventeen he began his teaching career as a grade teacher in St. Francis Xavier Grammar School, and at once began to work toward his A. B. degree in the Evening Session of the College of the City of New York. This was finally achieved in 1925, with *magna cum laude* and admission to Gamma Chapter of Phi Beta Kappa. But in the meanwhile he taught elementary and high school subjects in Xavier Grammar School, Regis High School, Fordham Preparatory School, and the Franklin School, and even spent a year in Havana as private tutor to the nephews of President Menocal of Cuba. He was also one of thirty-two recipients of a scholarship tour to Italy offered by the Italian Government in 1921 to American students of Italian birth or extraction.

In 1923, two years before completing his work for the A. B. degree in the Evening Session of City College, he was appointed instructor in Romance Languages and Latin in the College's Day Session and the College's preparatory high school, Townsend Harris. Having achieved his A. B. degree, he began work on his Ph. D. in Romance Philology and Comparative Linguistics in Columbia University. In 1932 he received the Ph. D. degree with the thesis "The Language of the Eighth-Century Texts in Northern France", which won him international renown. In 1937 Columbia appointed him Assistant Professor of Romance Philology. In 1947 he was made Associate Professor, and in 1952 Professor of Romance Philology, a post he still holds.

Among the honors and special appointments he has received are the George Washington Honor Medal from the Freedom Foundation at Valley Forge; the Cross of Cavaliere Ufficiale dell'Ordine del Merito of the Italian Republic; the appointment as Linguistic Consultant to the U. S. Army Language School in Monterey, California; the appointment as NATO Lecturer at the Universities of Lisbon and Coimbra, Portugal; the appointment as Andrew Mellon Visiting Professor of Languages at the University of Pittsburgh.

His writings include, to date, thirty-four published books of various types, but mostly dealing with language and languages. His *Story of Language,* published by Lippincott in 1949, was a Book-of-the-Month Club selection, and has appeared in British, French, Italian and Spanish editions. Among his works of deeper scholarship are, in addition to his doctoral dissertation, his *Italian Language, French Precursors of the Chanson de Roland, The Dictionary of Linguistics, One Language for the World, The Families of Words,* and *Voices of Man.* His *Languages for War and Peace,* later retitled *The World's Chief Languages,* marked the establishment of geolinguistics as a separate academic discipline; it is now in its fourth American and second British edition. Among his popularizations of language are *The Story of English, Language for Everybody, All About Language, Talking Your Way Around the World, The Book of Place Names, Our Names,* and the books of the *Getting Along in —* series (French, Italian, Spanish, German, Russian, Portuguese). His catholicity of interest is evidenced by two works on political and sociological topics, *The American Road to Peace* and *The Consumer's Manifesto,* and by two successful works of fiction, *Swords of Anjou* and *The Sparrows of Paris.* He is co-author of *First-Year French* and editor of Oliver Heatwole's *Comparative Grammar of French, Spanish and Italian,* as well as of Ada Boni's *Talisman Ita-*

lian Cook-Book. He is the translator of Vittorio de Fiori's *Mussolini, Man of Destiny,* and of François Mauriac's *Lettres Ouvertes.*

His articles and reviews run into the hundreds. The more popular ones have appeared in *The New York Times Magazine* and *Book Review, Saturday Evening Post, Holiday, Saturday Review, Reader's Digest, Catholic Digest, This Week, Coronet, Good Housekeeping, This Month, New Leader, Tomorrow, Town and Country, Think, Chicago Tribune, New York World-Telegram and Sun, Modern Age, Science Digest, Challenge, Hablemos, English Digest,* as well as *Sintesis* of Mexico City, *Hommes et Commerce* of Paris, *Lingue del Mondo* of Florence, and *UNESCO Courier.* His more scholarly articles (from which the current collection is drawn) have appeared in *Medium Aevum, Erasmus, Lingua Nostra, Modern Language Review, Modern Language Notes, Modern Language Journal, Romanic Review, Language, Word, Italica, Hispania, French Review, German Quarterly, Symposium, Speculum, American Speech.* His articles on various phases of education have appeared in *Education Digest, School and Society, AAUP Bulletin.*

His articles on specific language topics appear in a dozen encyclopedias, including Collier's, the Americana, the People's, and Funk and Wagnalls'. His recordings on medieval Romance literatures and Church Latin are produced by Folkways; his recorded courses in a variety of languages by Folkways, Funk & Wagnalls and David McKay.

Professor Pei has been a lecturer for such groups as the Foreign Policy Association, the English-Speaking Union, the Alliance Française, the Casa Italiana, the Hispanic Institute, the Foundation for Integrated Education, the Society for General Semantics, the America-Italy Society, the Italian Institute of Culture, and the Rotary Club. His more professional lectures have been given before various branches of the Modern Language Association, the Linguistic Circle of New York, and such colleges and universities as Hunter, Barnard, Wells, Wellesley, Cooper Union, New York University, Syracuse, Buffalo, Rochester, Adelphi, Hofstra, Marymount, Chatham, Washington of St. Louis, Omaha, Susquehanna, Kent, Temple, Greensboro, Yale, the Illinois Institute of Technology, the Tatnall School of Wilmington and the Vermont Academy. One of his recent lecture series was the Andrew Mellon Professorship Lectures on language, delivered at the Stephen Foster Memorial Chapel of the University of Pittsburgh.

He has appeared repeatedly on most radio and television stations in the New York metropolitan area, as well as in Pittsburgh, Los Angeles, San Francisco, St. Louis and elsewhere. Particularly significant have been his frequent appearances on the Voice of America's WRUL and University of the Air, and on Radio Free Europe, in a dozen European languages.

During World War Two, he collaborated with OSS and OWI in the preparation of linguistic projects connected with the war effort. At the same time, he constructed for the Coordinator of Inter-American Affairs a series of English lessons for Spanish speakers that was widely used in Latin America and later adapted by other government agencies for use in Europe, Asia and Africa.

1963 marks the fortieth anniversary of his college and university teaching, but the forty-sixth anniversary of his teaching career. On this occasion, his friends, colleagues and admirers have thought it fitting to present him with this brief volume of his own collected writings on philological topics, which appeared in various American periodicals that by reason of the war and the confusion of the postwar years in part failed to reach the reading public for which they were intended. The distribution to European libraries and scholars of the present volume is meant to fill that gap, and at the same time to honor one who has done much for the cause of languages, linguistics, and world understanding.

TABULA GRATULATORIA

Paul F. Angiolillo.
Harold von Arx.
Anna Balakian.
M. Banitt.
Sr. Virginia Belleggia, M. P. F.
Thomas G. Bergin.
Gerald A. Bertin.
Henry V. Besso.
Dorothy R. Brodin.
Victor Buescu.
Leon P. Calafiura.
Adrienne G. Cannon.
Rev. Luke M. Ciampi, O. F. M.
J. Reuben Clark, III.
Robert J. Clements.
Mario E. Cosenza.
Joseph B. Costanzo.
Elie Cristo-Loveanu.
Mrs. Cy Cutler.
Armand L. De Gaetano.
Ralph Paul de Gorog.
William F. J. De Jongh.
Anita-Louise De La Garza.
Rev. Dante del Fiorentino.
A. Michael De Luca.
Giulio de Petra.
Michelangelo De Rosa.
Joseph F. De Simone.
Giacomo Devoto.
Henri Diament.
Sylvia Klion Disenhof.
Filippo Donini.
Eugene Dorfman.
Henry Grattan Doyle.
Sister Eloise Thérèse.
Guido Errante.
Mischa H. Fayer.
Lena M. Ferrari.
Gertrude B. Fiertz.
Pasquale P. Filice.

Mary Finocchiaro.
Anna Fisher.
John Fisher.
Hans Flasche.
Joseph G. Fucilla.
Renée J. Fulton.
Paul A. Gaeng.
Frank M. Gatto.
Anthony Giammaresi.
Anthony M. Gisolfi.
Joseph V. Greco.
Oliver W. Heatwole.
David Heft.
Val Hempel.
Erik Hoder.
Edward J. Hoffman.
Theodore Huebener.
John P. Hughes.
Alfred Iacuzzi.
August C. Jennings.
Cesi Kellinger.
Charles F. Kirk.
Jack Kolbert.
Harry Kurz.
Ferdinand M. LaBastille.
Milan S. LaDu.
Donald W. Lee.
Jesse Levitt.
Leonard Lieberman.
Mira B. Lomont.
Maristella Lorch.
Rosemary Lucente.
Archibald T. MacAllister.
Duncan MacDougald, Jr.
Howard R. Marraro.
Antonio Martel.
Carlota Martel.
José Martel.
Ferdinando D. Maurino.
Dorothy M. McGhee.

TABULA GRATULATORIA

John L. McWilliams.
F. de Mello Moser.
Alberto Menarini.
Ramón Menéndez-Pidal.
Marie C. Mengers.
Edmond A. Méras.
Camillo P. Merlino.
Nella Meyer.
Bruno Migliorini.
Nicholas J. Milella.
Bruce Milo.
Angelo Monteverdi.
Žarko Muljačić.
René F. Muller.
Louis H. Naylor.
Fedor I. Nikanov.
Sergio J. Pacifici.
Louis A. Pagnucco.
Manuel de Paiva Boleo.
Remigio U. Pane.
George C. Pappageotes.
Carlo Pellegrini.
José Ângelo Peral Ribeiro.
Emilio Peruzzi.
Frieda N. Politzer.
Robert L. Politzer.
Lillian Polstein.
Anna Potop.
Alexander R. Prista.

Oreste F. Pucciani.
Olga Ragusa.
Salvatore Ramondino.
Olga Razzari.
Louise Barbara Richardson.
Gerhard Rohlfs.
David Romey.
Carol Rosen.
Gene M. Sackrin.
Peter Sammartino.
Louis F. Sas.
S. Eugene Scalia.
Edward F. Sciorsci.
Ralph W. Scott.
Alfred Senn.
Barton Sholod.
Charles S. Singleton.
T. Lane Skelton.
T. O'Connor Sloane, III.
James P. Soffietti.
Ernest V. Speranza.
Abraham Tauber.
Pauline Taylor.
Salvatore R. Tocci.
Vito G. Toglia.
University of Pittsburgh.
Josephine Vallerie.
Antonina Serio Vella.
Yvonne R. Mitchell Weber.
Martin Zwart.

1

OLD FRENCH DEMONSTRATIVES

The etymology of OF *icist, icil, ici, iço* from *ecce + iste, ille, hic, hoc* is widely accepted without discussion by Romance scholars.[1]

The phonetic difficulties presented by the initial *i* of the OF forms are generally ignored. Yet the presence of an *i* not derived from Lat. $\bar{\imath}$ in the initial syllable of OF words is an extremely rare phenomenon.[2] Bourciez[3] claims that the change of $e > i$, which occurs in Italy, does not appear in Gaul; Guarnerio[4] claims the change $e > i$ for parts of Italy, Moldavia, the Morvan and Walloon dialects and Asturias, but states[5] that in French this change occurs only before *n* or *l*. The same statement is made by Meyer-Lübke.[6] The latter author, who carefully refrains from offering the etymology *ecce + iste, ille, hic*, either in his Grammaire or in his Rom. et. Wb., refutes by implication the theory of a possible double retro-

---

[1] Cr. Diez, Et. Wb. d. rom. Sprachen, s. vv. *questo, quello, qui*; Bourciez, Eléments de linguistique romane 235, 251, 341; Grandgent, Introduction to Vulgar Latin 35-6; Nyrop, Gram. hist. de la langue fr. 2.391-402; Körting, Lat.-rom. Wb.; Bloch, Dict. ét. de la langue fr.; Brunot, Hist. de la langue fr., 1.192-3; Anglade; Gram. de l'ancien fr. 97-8, 147; Stappers, Dict. synoptique d'étymologie fr., Clédat, Manuel de phon. et de morph. rom. 88.
[2] *lion* < *leonem*, caused by hiatus; *ciment* < *caementum*, caused by initial palatal; Anglade 28.
[3] Op. cit., 153, 288.
[4] Fonologia romanza 338-9.
[5] Op. cit. 352.
[6] Grammaire des langues romanes 1.306.

gressive assimilation (*ecce iste* > *ecce ęstī* > *eccist* > *icist*) by a discussion [7] of the dissimilative tendencies of *ī* (*vīcīnus* > *vęcino*, *dīvīnare* > *dęvinare*, etc.) as borne out by OF development.

Diez, in his Et. Wb. d. rom. Sprachen, after presenting the possibility of *icelui* and *icelei* > *ipsi lui* and *ipsi illi ei*, appearing in the formularies of Marculfus and Mabillon, gives up the attempt on phonetic grounds (OF *c* cannot represent Lat. *s*, as proved by Picard *chelui, ichi*), and reverts to the *ecce* etymology, despite its obvious phonetic shortcomings, offering as proof a rare construction appearing in medieval writers *(parentes ecce habeo multos)*.

Few other scholars attempt to solve the problem of the initial *i*. Anglade calls it prothetic: an unsatisfactory explanation, in view of the fact that the prothetic vowel in French is *e*, not *i*, and that nowhere else does prothesis appear in words of this type, beginning with palatalized *c*. Bourciez [8] and Clédat [9] both advance the hypothesis of the influence of the following palatalized *c* for the vowel change; but such influence is without parallel.

Schwan-Behrens is the only Romance scholar who faces the situation squarely. He states: [10] 'Une explication satisfaisante manque encore pour le premier *i* d'*icil* et d'*icist*', and again: [11] 'L'explication de l'*i* initial de la forme primitive présente également des difficultés, si l'on compare les transformations d'*ekke*, là où il apparaît comme mot indépendant' (*ekke* > *ez*).

In view of these apparently insoluble phonetic difficulties, a thorough investigation of the Vulgar and Medieval Latin texts of the 7th, 8th, 9th, and 10th centuries would seem to point to the possibility of a combination of *hīc* (either the adverb, or a standardized form of the demonstrative, extended to all cases, numbers, and genders) with *iste, ille*, and *hic*, the compound being phonetico-syntactically treated as a single word, with palatalization of an intervocalic *c* placed between two front vowels (unlike *hoc ille* > *oïl*; cf. Grandgent 112 for the general retention of final gutturals in Vulgar Latin, and compare *plácere > *plagere > *plaiere > *plaire* and *placé-*

---

[7] Grammaire 1.303.
[8] Phonétique française 129.
[9] Manuel de phonétique 104.
[10] Grammaire de l'ancien français 69.
[11] Op. cit. 195.

re > *platsere > *plaitsieir > *plaisir* for the double treatment of gutturals in Fr.). In the case of *hic hoc* > *iço* the formation would be due to analogy. This analogy would seem at least as reasonable as that by which etymological dictionaries explain such formations as *itel, itant, idonc* (< *talem, tantum, deumquam* with initial *i* from analogy of *icist, icil, ici*). No analogical explanation is needed for *itel, itant, idonc,* if an invariable *hic* is accepted as the first member of the compound, and OF *issi*, usually explained as from *aeque sic*, can equally well be referred to *hic sic*. A real economy in the use of the doubtful analogical factor is thus effected by accepting *hic* in the place of *ecce*.

Combinations such as *ecce ille, ecce iste,* which appear in Plautus,[12] are not in evidence in the texts of the Vulgar Latin period; these on the contrary display, particularly from the 7th century on, a double use of *hic* which appears to point, on the one hand, to an extension of the standardized masc. sing. nom. (or the adverb), and on the other hand, to an ever more frequent combination with *iste* in the function of a true demonstrative (*ille* having lost demonstrative force by virtue of its frequent use as an article).

Gregory of Tours uses *hic* for *haec* (fem. sg.).[13] Vielliard, in her discussion of the Merovingian charters,[14] speaks of the extension of the form *hic* to the fem. singular and plural, particularly in those annotations on the reverse of the documents which more currently betray the spoken language. The same phenomenon is reported by Delisle.[15] In my own work,[16] I have reported frequent cases of a similar use (*hic sunt carctas, hic est emunitas,* etc.). It would therefore appear that there was a tendency, attested since the 6th century and becoming more widespread in the 7th and 8th, to extend the use of *hic* (adverb or demonstrative?) to cover the functions of other declensional forms, particularly *haec*.

---

[12] Grandgent 35-6.
[13] Bonnet, Le latin de Grégoire de Tours 387.
[14] La langue des diplômes royaux et chartes privées de l'époque mérovingienne, Paris, 1927, 145-6.
[15] Authentiques de reliques de l'époque mérovingienne, Mélanges de l'école française de Rome, 1884, 4.3.
[16] The Language of the Eighth-Century Texts in Northern France, N. Y., 1932, 173.

The combination of forms of *hic* with *iste* is strongly attested in the latter part of the 8th century, a formative and creative period for OF, and in the 9th and 10th centuries, when we may suppose that the etymological feeling of the original derivation of OF forms was not yet lost. I have shown [17] such expressions as *hanc donatione ista, contra hanc epistulam donacionis ista*, appearing in the latter part of the 8th century. Similar, but far more numerous forms are reported by Slijper, [18] who states in connection with his 8th century mss.: '*Hic* saepissime conjunctum invenies cum *iste*; *contra hanc securitate ista* passim, *hec vindicio ista*', etc. Beszard [19] reports for his 9th century mss.: 'Il est du reste fréquent de trouver *iste* accompagnant un autre démonstratif: *hanc cartolam ista, hanc cessione ista*, etc. Ces expressions pourraient être considérées comme relevant de la syntaxe; nous les mentionnons ici parce qu'elles rappellent de bien près les dém. doubles *ecce hic, ecce ille, ecce iste*, etc., qui sont les thèmes étymologiques de nombreux démonstratifs romans.' Morel [20] reports an abundance of *hic* + *iste* forms in the Cluny texts.

A more extensive investigation of the original documents of Tardif [21] and of the documents of Cluny [22] for the 8th, 9th, and 10th centuries brings to light the following facts:

In the royal deeds of Tardif, the scribes of the king's court, trained in the use of Latin since the reform of Pepin and Charlemagne, display better care in their handling of the demonstratives. The demonstrative function taken over by *ipse* in the 7th and 8th centuries (in the sense of 'the aforesaid') is to a large extent replaced in the 9th by *iste, hic,* and (more rarely) *ille* and *idem*. The combination of *hic* and *iste* is rare, though we have *presens donatio ista* (101) in 848, and the two words occurring in direct contact: *hec ista* (153) about the year 1000. On the other hand, we have an interesting extension of *hic* (142) in 916: *hic sancto loco dare*; and, toward the end of the 10th century, when we may suppose that the etymologi-

---

[17] Op. cit. 198, 201.
[18] De Formularum Andecavensium Latinitate Disputatio, Amsterdam, 1906, 115.
[19] La langue des formules de Sens, Paris, 1910, 32.
[20] Ecole des chartes, positions des thèses de 1914, 77-82.
[21] Monuments historiques, Paris, 1866.
[22] Bernard, Recueil des chartes de l'abbaye de Cluny, Paris, 1876, I-II.

cal sense of the derivation of *icist* was beginning to be lost, such combinations as *illi ipsi fratres, his ipsis hic, eis ipsis, illis ipsis* (153).

On the other hand, the private documents of Cluny, written by less cultured scribes, display an impressive series of combinations throughout the 9th and 10th centuries: *hanc vindicione ista*, 845 (8); *anc vindicione ista*, 870 (16); *ec condonacio ista*, 903 (90); and countless others. Erroneous uses of forms of *hic*, such as *oc vindicione ista*, 906 (210); *ec dotalio isto*, 928 (177); *ec scamius istus*, 920 (210); *anc dotalicio isto*, 928 (335); *ec ipso campo*, 915 (187), attest the loss of declensional sense for *hic* which we might expect if *hic* had been previously standardized in speech to the exclusion of all other declensional forms. In an especially poorly written document of the year 881 (29), we find the two words in direct contact: *hanc ista vindictione, ehc ista vindictio*.

It is worthy of note that in the vast majority of cases where *hic* and *iste* are combined, the two forms are separated by the interposition of the noun. This is possibly a conventionalized concession made by the scribes to classical usage, a compromise between the directly combined *hic iste* of their speech and the knowledge existing in their minds that classical Latin regularly makes use of a single demonstrative. From the outset of the *hic* + *iste* vogue, in the second half of the 8th century, until the end of the 10th, it is only exceptionally that the two forms appear in direct contact. But this, occurring as it does at a period when the scribes had been definitely made conscious of Classical Latin by the Carolingian Renaissance, is not a factor of sufficient importance to cause us to reject the theory, attested by the extension of *hic* since the 6th century and by the combining tendencies of *hic* and *iste* since the 8th, that it may have been a standardized *hic*, in close phonetico-syntactic combination with *iste, ille, hic,* and *hoc*, that gave rise to OF *icist, icil, ici, iço*, rather than an *ecce* which is at variance with the phonetic development of French.

This hypothesis, resting as it does upon evidence supplied by the texts of the Vulgar and Medieval Latin periods, points once again to the importance of a thorough study of those texts when attempting to solve difficult or controversial points in Romance development.

Languge, XII (1936).

11

FRENCH 'ICIL'

In his criticism (*Modern Language Review*, XXXII, p. 83) of my article on Old French demonstratives (*Language*, XII, p. 48), Edwin H. Tuttle appears to have misunderstood one of my statements. I advanced *hoc ille* > *oïl* as an exception to the general rule, which may, however, well have been due to original heavier stress on *hoc*. It is possible that my referring to two front vowels may have led to the misunderstanding, though the example of the double development of *placere* which immediately followed might have made the meaning clear.

As for your correspondent's main contention that *hic ille* should have made a form with *dz* and later voiced *s*, it may be pointed out that such treatment is by no means universal (*recimer, recivt*—Léger; *deces*—Alexis; *receit*—Roland; also note: *deci*—Aliscans; *de ci*—Couronnement de Louis; *desci*—Roman de Troie; *dessi*—Richard le Beau, indicating some confusion of intervocalic *c* (*ts*) and *s* sounds at this period, if we accept the commonly claimed derivation from *de sic*).

But even if we were to accept the writer's assertion that voiced *dz* > *z* (*s*) is the universal outcome in groups of the vowel + *c* + accented front vowel type, he himself suplies an excellent explanation for the retention of the hard sound in the demonstratives when he states that *cil* is at least as old as *icil*. In words in which apheresis was so early and frequent, it stands to reason that the consonant would receive initial rather than intervocalic treatment, even where the initial vowel was retained.

Lastly, the explanations which the writer offers for *icil* appear to leave the question completely unanswered. If *cil* < *ecce ĭlle* is the older form, and *icil* is 'a French word-group, with French *i* prefixed to *cil*', we should like to know whence this French *i* comes. If *icil* is older, and represents a 'blending of **ecil* with *i*', or 'a phonetic reduction of *i *ecil*, with absorption of weak-stressed *e* by the more strongly stressed *i*', we are still left in doubt as to the origin of the *i*, especially in those very numerous forms (*iceste, icele, icez, iceles, iço, idonc, itel*, etc.) where we cannot attribute the change to the influence of an original Classical or Vulgar Latin final $\bar{\imath}$, and are consequently compelled to resort to no less than two doubtful assimilations (*ecce *ellī* > *eccil* > *icil*), followed by an entire series of equally doubtful analogies (*icil, icele*, etc.; then *idonc, itant, itel*).

Hic, which has more support from documentary evidence than *ecce*, eliminates these vague hypothetical processes and supplies a clear phonetic derivation whose benefits may even be extended to the second *i* of *icist* and *icil* (*hīc *ellī, hīc *estī*, with assimilative force exerted upon the stressed vowel from two directions instead of one).

Modern Language Review, XXXIII (1938).

III

ACCUSATIVE OR OBLIQUE?

A. H. Schutz's review of my book,[1] appearing in *Language*,[2] brings again to the fore a time-honored controversy in the field of Romance Philology, to wit, whether the oblique case of Old French and Old Provençal, as well as the single case of other Romance languages, is the direct descendant of the Classical Latin accusative, with the other oblique cases of Classical Latin thrown into the discard; or the result of a merger of Classical Latin accusative, ablative and dative, brought about by the phonetic equivalence of the singular endings in two of the three major declensions, and then gradually extended, by a syntactical process of analogy, to cover the dative singular of the first declension, the genitive singular of the three declensions, and those plural forms which could not phonetically coalesce.

Inasmuch as upon the correct interpretation of this controversial point there hangs not only a clearer understanding of the linguistic processes that went on in the Vulgar Latin period, but also an evaluation of the methods whereby linguistic processes and problems in this field have been approached, a condensed restatement of the theories involved and of the old and new evidence at hand is in order.

Diez's theory of the Latin accusative as the progenitor of Ro-

---

[1] *The Language of the Eighth-Century Texts in Northern France*, N. Y., 1932.
[2] XI, 1 (Mar. 1935), pp. 47-49.
[3] *Sull'origine dell'unica forma flessionale del nome italiano*, Pisa, 1872.

mance single and oblique forms was first challenged by D'Ovidio, [3] who claimed that the single case of words such as It. *buono, morte,* Sp. *bueno, muerte* does not represent a particular case of the classical declension that prevailed because of some logical or intentional reason, but is rather a phonetic outcome of the fusion of the two oblique cases (accusative and ablative) which prevailed in the spoken language of the Empire; that universally, in the case of the singular of the first declension, and extensively in regions, like Italy and Roumania, where final -*s* disappeared, this coalition was joined by the nominative; and that a similar process occurred in the plural, save that there, where phonetic equivalence was impossible, the movement was aided by analogy, working along lines of least resistance, *bono(s),* for instance, being overcome in It. by the coalition of *boni* and *boni(s).*

This new theory, at the time of its appearance, aroused a storm of opposition. Ascoli's defense of D'Ovidio's theory, [4] based primarily upon the development of imparisyllabic third-declension neuter nouns in the Romance languages, was fiercely assailed by the exponents of the accusative thesis. [5] And with that, the discussion of necessity came to a halt, both schools having exhausted their ammunition, which consisted of deductive retracements from the Romance languages to a hypothetical Vulgar Latin or to attested classical forms, with little or no reference to the written documents of the period involved.

It was only at a considerably later date that the use of a different method of approach began to cast additional light upon this highly interesting problem. I have listed [6] the findings in this connection of authors who at various times have made a direct study of the Vulgar Latin documents. The confusion prevailing in the minds of earlier research workers brought up on the Diezian theory of the accusative is progressively cleared away, until we find, in the case of three authors [7] who had the additional advantage of work-

---

[4] Archivio Glottologico, II, 416-438; III, 466-467; IV, 398-402; X, 262-269.

[5] W. Meyer-Lübke, *Grammaire des langues romanes,* II, 8-11, 14-16, 19, 44-47.

[6] *Op. cit.,* 208-210.

[7] Haag, *Die Latinität Fredegars,* 1898, pp. 40-42, 65; Schramm, *Sprachliches zur Lex Salica,* 1911, pp. 84-87; Taylor, *The Latinity of the Liber*

ing with comparatively late texts of the seventh and eighth centuries, that a firm stand is taken in favor of the oblique case. To the findings of these investigators, I have added my own,[8] fortified by statistical tables which show, among other things, "in the singular, 599 oblique forms, with the apparently ablative endings *-a, -o, -e,* used in the accusative function, with 61 inverse accusative forms used in the ablative or dative function; 269 apparently correct accusative forms and 828 apparently correct ablative forms", and advanced the conclusion that "the bulk of evidence in our own and other texts of the Seventh and Eighth Centuries points very definitely to the creation of a single oblique case with the endings *-a, -o* and *-e* (plural *-as, -os* or *-is, -es* or *-is*)".

Against this mass of inductive, statistical evidence in favor of the oblique case, Schutz resurrects the arguments used by Meyer-Lübke and Nyrop against Ascoli and D'Ovidio.

While it might, on the one hand, be argued that the new proof derived from the Vulgar Latin texts is in itself conclusive enough to settle the discussion, we must not leave out of our reckoning the fact that many philologists, nurtured in a school which refused to see in the written documents of the sixth, seventh and eighth centuries anything but the attempt of a cultured class to write Classical Latin, cast grave doubt upon the value of such evidence, and adhere to the creed that "what is interesting in a semi-learned document is not what survives from Classical Latin, but simply what predicts the nascent Romance languages", which means that only those features of the documents are to be accepted which coincide with the deductive findings of the pioneers of Romance Philology. A single sporadic occurrence of a Romance feature in the midst of hundreds of classical forms is to this school of thought conclusive evidence that the Romance feature in question held undisputed sway in the spoken tongue, instead of being accepted as evidence of the fact that the language was *beginning* to change; while, on the other hand, thousands of irregularities of the same description and of a

---

Historiae Francorum, 1924, pp. 12-13, 64-97. Taylor, in particular, defends the oblique case with statistics showing a ratio of 200 to 15 in favor of oblique case-endings. In another work (*Chrestomathy of Vulgar Latin,* pp. 15-16, 54-57), Taylor, in collaboration with Muller, traces the oblique case from the time of Gregory of Tours to the Oaths of Strasbourg.

[8] *Op. cit.,* pp. 213-232.

highly significant nature, which tend to show in what direction the language was actually changing, are to be summarily dismissed because they do not fit in with hitherto accepted notions.

Arguments of a deductive type being the only ones acceptable to the followers of this school of thought, a review of such arguments, accompanied by certain novel considerations, is in order.

* * *

The accusative theory is upheld by its supporters [9] on the following grounds:

1. Monosyllabic words with final -*m* (Fr. *rien, mon, ton, son*; Sp. *quien*; It. *speme*) indicate the accusative form.

2. Logudorese, which keeps final -*o* and -*u* distinct (*otto, amo,* but *chentu, cantamus*), has a form ending in -*u* for second-declension nouns and adjectives (*oru, chelu, duru, plenu*).

3. Various Italian dialects which admit of umlaut indicate that the final vowel causing the umlaut in the singular is -*u*, not -*o*.

4. Imparisyllabic neuter third-declension nouns develop into the Romance languages from the accusative, not from the ablative form.

Before taking up each of these points in detail, it will be well to offer one important consideration: for forms in which phonetic equivalence is impossible, proponents of the accusative theory, in order to establish their point, find themselves in the necessity of disproving all, or practically all ablative survivals; proponents of the oblique or mixed-case theory, on the other hand, can concede any number of accusative survivals, provided they can show at the same time a considerable body of ablative survivals to counterbalance the former. Their theory being that accusative and ablative (and, we may add, dative) merged in the singular where phonetically possible, their logical stand is that where such phonetic fusion was not possible, a conflict arose between the two forms, one or the other being compelled to give way. This conflict, arising at a time when the bonds that held the Empire together were loosened,

---

[9] Meyer-Lübke, *op. cit.*; Nyrop, *Grammaire historique de la langue française*, II, 229.

could perfectly well have a different solution in different portions of the Romance area, Italian, for instance, preferring the accusative form of a given word while Spanish chose the ablative.

This important point of discussion having been established, the various accusative-theory arguments may be taken up in detail.

No. 1 is incontrovertible, so far as it goes. If we establish it as a phonetic law that final *-m* survived in monosyllabic words, we shall find no difficulty whatsoever in deriving *rien, mon, quien, speme*, etc., from accusative forms; but we may, on the other hand, express some surprise at the fact that Italian dialects show possessive forms *mo, ma, to, ta, so, sa*, and that French has *ma, ta, sa* without a final nasal. Are these to be regarded, in view of the phonetic rule, as ablative forms, or are we to say that the retention of final *-m* in monosyllables is a capricious and arbitrary phenomenon? Spanish *alguien* < *aliquem* also shows definite retention of final accusative *-m*, in a polysyllabic word. Shall we describe this as a sporadic occurrence, attribute it to the analogy of *quien*, or attempt to balance it against the countless forms in which final *-m* disappears? It would seem that the retention of final *-m* in the cases above cited simply points to the survival of *certain* accusative forms, and nothing more.

No exception can be taken to no. 2, but here again it seems that more is assumed as a conclusion than the evidence warrants. Granted that Logudorese keeps final *-o* and *-u* separate, we are faced with the only Romance region in which a phonetic conflict between second declension accusative and ablative was possible. Conflicts have a way of coming to an ultimate settlement. In the Logudorese area (roughly one-third of Sardinia) the conflict was apparently solved in favor of the accusative. Does this warrant our assuming that the same solution took place in the remainder of Romance territory, where phonetic conditions did not call for a drastic triumph of one form over the other? We know little concerning the nature and duration of the struggle that may have taken place in central Sardinia between two forms that could not phonetically coincide, but it is quite possible that for centuries the issue hung in the balance, and that *-u* and *-o* forms coexisted side by side before the levelling forces of analogy swung the scales in favor of *-u* forms that may, at the outset, have had only a slender majority. Certainly

ACCUSATIVE OR OBLIQUE?

the hesitation reported by Wagner[10] between final -o and -u in a south central Sardinian variety which is a next-door neighbor to Logudorese, and the occurrence of numerous -o endings (*domo, sero,* etc.) reported by Meyer-Lübke,[11] and attributed by him and Wagner to isolated or "crystallized" ablative survivals, both lend favor to the theory that it was only as a result of a long struggle that -o endings succumbed to -u endings in the only section where they could not merge.[12] At any rate, the triumph of the accusative in central Sardinia can be taken as proof of only one fact: that in the sole instance where the phonetic fusion of the oblique cases was not possible, the accusative proved stronger; and this in a single region of Romance territory, very limited in extent and almost severed from communication with the rest of the Latin-speaking world at the very time when the all-important process of declensional change was beginning. Additional inferences derived from this fact seem arbitrary and unwarranted.

No. 3 is an argument of much the same type. Meyer-Lübke[13] undertakes to prove that where umlaut appears in certain south central Italian dialects, the final vowel causing the umlaut is -u, not -o. Without rejecting this contention, it is only fair to point out that the identical argument is advanced by Ascoli[14] in support of his own inferences; he presents a series of examples from French,

---

[10] *Lautlehre der südsardischen Mundarten,* p. 17.

[11] *Zur Kenntniss der Altlogudoresischen,* p. 13.

[12] A careful examination of the earliest Sardinian documents seems to indicate that in Logudorese, as well as in the rest of the Sardinian area, the conflict still persisted in the 11th and 12th centuries. The earliest Log. charter (1080-1085; Monaci, *Crestomazia italiana dei primi secoli,* pp. 4-5) presents the following forms in -o: *Mariano; sso* (< *sum*); *ipsoro* (< *ipsorum*); *Bernardu de Conizo.* That portion of the Condaghe di San Pietro di Silki (middle of the 12th century) which is given by Monteverdi in his *Testi volgari italiani anteriori al Duecento* (pp. 42-49) contains: *nontho; suo; domo; Sorso.* A charter from Arborea previous to 1112 (Monteverdi, pp. 34-36) bears: *potestu suo; domo; ipsoro; co* (< *cum*); *iscrinio ferreo.* Campidanese charters from Cagliari (1070-1080, 1089-1103; Monteverdi, pp. 19-23, 29-31) contain a large number of -o forms, some of them alternating with -u (σσάντω ησπήαιτο-σσπήθιτου σάντου; φίλιο-φίλιου), despite the fact that Campid. has since then gone over completely to the forms in -u. By way of contrast, a Campidanese document of a later period (1212; Monaci, pp. 28-29) shows the full triumph of -u.

[13] *Op. cit.,* II, 19, 44-47.

[14] *Arch. Glott.,* X, 260-271.

Provençal and Rhetian in which the umlaut appears to have been produced by a final -*o* to the exclusion of -*u*; and he even produces doublets (Prov. *nid, niu*) in which one form is claimed to be an ablative, the other an accusative survival.

We now come to what appears to be the crux of the question, the survival of accusative and ablative forms in imparisyllabic neuter nouns of the third declension, where accusative and ablative could not phonetically merge, and the conflict had to be solved along lines of individual choice. Reference must here again be made to the two giants of the declensional combat, Ascoli and Meyer-Lübke.[15] The former presents a large number of ablative survivals, sets them off against an approximately equal number of accusative survivals, and claims that this indecision of the Romance languages in cases where phonetic fusion was impossible proves the oblique-case theory. Meyer-Lübke undertakes, in his refutation, to destroy, one by one, Ascoli's ablative examples, by claiming, in some cases, transfer from the neuter to the masculine gender; in others, that the forms alleged by Ascoli are learned; in others, that Ascoli's forms were reconstructed from the plural or from verbs; in others, that a Vulgar form coexisted side by side with the attested form. Here and there, an ablative form presents itself for which no explanation is possible, at which times it is labeled as exceptional and unaccounted for.

* * *

A complete study of the Romance descendants of 135 third declension imparisyllabic neuter nouns appearing in Meyer-Lübke[16] and Körting,[17] including both attested and hypothetical forms, but exclusive of Greek nouns in -*ma*, which were probably felt to be foreign and underwent special treatment, casts additional light upon the matter, despite the fact that the majority of the more striking examples have already been used by Ascoli or Meyer-Lübke or both in the course of their controversy.

---

[15] Cf. notes 4 and 5.
[16] *Romanisches etymologisches Wörterbuch.*
[17] *Lateinisch-romanisches Wörterbuch.*

In classifying these nouns, we find that they fall into three general types, each of which presents peculiar possibilities of development. They are: I. nouns that are monosyllabic in the nominative-accusative and dissyllabic in the other oblique cases (*far, farre*); II. polysyllabic nouns that present a shift of stress from the nom.-acc. to the other oblique cases (*animal, animale*); III. polysyllabic nouns in which the position of the stress is retained throughout (*caput, capite*). The last class, including the '-*men,* '-*mine* group, is by far the most numerous.

I. 1. -*ác,* -*ácte.*

lac—Romance descendants of this word come from the longer form, with the single exception of Vegliote *lik*; frequent occurrences of *lacte* in the nom. and *lactem* in the acc. in classical authors, however, indicate a shift of ending or of gender which renders the value of this example extremely doubtful.

I. 2. -*ál,* -*ále.*

sal—This form, variously appearing as masculine and neuter (Ennius, *sale,* neut.), is of no value.

I. 3. -*ár,* -*árre.*

far—It. *farro, farre* and Log. *farre* give plain indication of ablative survival. This form is not mentioned by Ascoli, while Meyer-Lübke, dealing only with It. and Sp. *farro,* and overlooking the -*e* forms of It. and Log., claims that they are based on the analogy of *vas* > *vasum, os* > *ossum,* further claiming that the *f* of the Sp. form indicates learned influence. Even granting this, the presence of the forms in -*e,* with double *r* preceding, cannot be accounted for save by ablative survival (addition of epenthetic -*e* would not cause the doubling of the preceding consonant; cf. It. and Log. development of *cor*).

I. 4. -*ás,* -*áse.*

vas—While It. *vaso* is obviously due to the shift *vas* > *vasum* indicated by Meyer-Lübke, the archaic It. form *vase* seems to indicate an ablative survival. Phonetically, instead of adding epenthetic -*e, vas* should have given *vai in It. [18]

I. 5. -*él,* -*élle.*

---

[18] Grandgent, *From Latin to Italian,* 94; D'Ovidio & Meyer-Lübke, *Grammatica storica della lingua e dei dialetti italiani,* p. 112; Guarnerio, *Fonologia romanza,* p. 524.

fel, mel—Here we have accusative survivals in Roum. *fiere, miere*, It. *fiele, miele*, Log. *fele, mele*, all with addition of epenthetic *-e*. The only clear-cut descendant of the ablative is It. *felle*, but this double development of *fel* in It. is significant.

I. 6. *-én, -éne.*

ren—Despite Körting's claim, and the OLog. form *rena*, it is extremely doubtful that this noun was neuter. If it was, OSp. *réne* and Pt. *rine* would be evidence of ablative survival.

I. 7. *-ér, -ére.*

ver—No conclusive evidence can be drawn from Roum. *vară*, ONeap. *vera*, which seem to come from the plural.

I. 8. *-ór, -órde.*

cor—Meyer-Lübke claims that this form took epenthetic *-e* in It. and Roum. No survivor of *corde* appearing, this statement may be accepted. This development, however, may justly be contrasted with that of *far*.

I. 9. *-ús, -úre.*

jus, pus—In the sense of "law", OSp. *jur* is combated by Meyer-Lübke on the ground that it is a learned form derived from *de jure, in jure*, while It. *giure* is claimed by Körting to be learned. In the sense of "broth", OF *jus* is evidently an accusative survival. *Pus* has as its popular descendant Abruzzian *purə*, which can only be an ablative survival.

In conclusion, the monosyllabic group, small as it is, indicates an approximately equal number of apparent accusative and ablative survivals, with the forms *farre, vase, purə*, which cannot be eliminated on any reasonable ground save by assuming hypothetical **farre-is, *vase-is, *pure-is*, for which no evidence appears; and one case of double development within the same language (It. *felle, fiele*).

* * *

Before undertaking a discussion of the nouns that show a shift of stress from the nom.-acc. to the other oblique cases, it will be well to mention that Ascoli overlooks them altogether in his demonstration, while Meyer-Lübke disposes of them by claiming that Vulgar Latin developed a longer nom.-acc. form (*áltar* > *altáre*), which was the only one kept save in It. *baccáno* < *bacchánal*. One may well wonder why It., which is said to be so prone to adding epenthetic -*e* in other cases, should prove to be the sole exception to this tendency. Grandgent [19] claims that the inverse phenomenon, namely, the dropping of final -*e* after liquids, took place in Vulgar Latin.

II. 1. '-*al*, -*ále*.

ánimal, bacchánal, cervícal—The first of these nouns has a variety of descendants in the northern It. dialects (Valsessa *rimá*, Piacenza *limál*, Parma *nimál*, Belluno *muñál*, Reggio *nimä*), as well as in Rhetian (Obwald. *armál*, Friulan *nemál*). These forms, which are universally ablative in appearance, contrast strongly with It. *baccáno* < *bacchánal*, which appears to be of accusative origin; while in Neap. *červekalə*, Valsessa *šervigá* and Prov. *cervigal* we return once more to ablative forms.

II 2. '-*ar*, -*áre*.

cóchlear, exémplar, lúminar, pugíllar, tórcular—In the first of these examples, the fact that *cochleare* is also attested deprives Fr. *cuiller*, Prov. *cuilher*, Sp. *cuchar* and Pt. *colhar* of their value. OF *essemplaire*, in addition to being a semi-learned form, appears to be derived from the plural. *Luminar* is the only classical form for the noun, though *luminare* is offered by both Körting and Meyer-Lübke as the progenitor of Venetian *luminal*, Sp. *umbral*, OPt. *lomear*, Roum. *lumanară*, It. and Log. *luminare*. Semi-learned Roum. *pughilar* and Sp. *pugilar* are doubtful examples of ablative survival. Forez *trul'á* and Sp. *trujal* are popular ablative derivatives.

II. 3. '-*ec*, -*éce*.

állec—Despite the existence of a masc.-fem. form *álex-écis*, this form is of interest by reason of the fact that in It. *álece, álice* and Sic. *áleci* an accusative derivation is suggested, while Sp. *aléce, haléche* are either ablative derivatives or come from the masc.-fem. form.

II. 4. '-*er*, -*ínere*.

íter—OF *erre, oirre*, OMilanese *edre, edro*, and It. *erre* in *perder l'erre* (offered by Körting but not generally accepted) are accusative derivatives. It. *itinere* seems a learned word.

---

[19] *Introduction to Vulgar Latin*, 242.

It may be said conclusion that nouns of the accent-shifting type tend to the ablative form, but that there is a sufficient number of accusative survivals (*baccáno, álece, erre*) to indicate that the conflict existed here as well as elsewhere, and to refute Meyer-Lübke's sweeping statement concerning the passage from a short to a longer nom.-acc. form, such passage being attested only for some nouns of the *'-ar* type.

* * *

The third class of nouns (polysyllabic with no accent-shift) is, by reason both of its numbers and its variety, the most fruitful of discussion, and Ascoli, disregarding the valuable possibilities offered by the other two classes enumerated above, concentrated his efforts upon it.

III. 1. a. *'-ar, '-are*.

bústar—Uncertainty concerning the quantity of the *a* in the oblique cases may lead us to classify this noun with II. 2 (*torcular*, etc.), in which case Sp. *bostar* and Pt. *bostal* would either be of ablative origin or accounted for by the general passage from a short to a long form in the nom.-acc. postulated by Meyer-Lübke for all nouns of this class. If the *a*, as appears probable, was short in all cases, we are faced with a shift of accent in Sp. and Pt. which still leaves us in doubt, though *bústare* > *bostáre appears the most likely hypothesis.

III. 1. b. *'-ar, '-ate*.

hépar—Here we have Judeo-French *ebre, evre* and It. *epa* showing accusative survival, while Judeo-French *ebede*, It. *épate* and possibly Roum. *hípotă* point to the ablative. This interesting form, displaying double survival in the same languages, is neglected by both Ascoli and Meyer-Lübke.

III. 2. a. *'-en, '-ine* (exclusive of *-men* forms).

inguen, pécten, póllen, sánguen—It. *inguine* points to ablative survival; derivation from the plural is indicated by Tarentine *enčida*, Log. *imbena*, Pt. *ingua*; while Engadine *engle*, OF *aigne*, Prov. *lengue* and Sp. *ingle* are of doubtful derivation. *Pecten*, claimed by Körting as a neuter, and cited by Ascoli as having produced a double form in Log. (*petten, pettene*), appears elsewhere as a masculine, and can hardly be accepted as fair evidence. In the case of *pollen* and *sanguen*, the presence of concomitant masculine forms (*pollis, sanguis*) invalidates in part the evidence of Log. *podda* vs. It. *polline*, Tarentine *pónila*, Lecce *pónnula*, Log. *poddine*, Campid. *poddini*, and of Roum. *sînge*, It. *sangue*, Fr. *sang*, etc. vs. It. *sanguine*, Log. *sambene*, Sp. *sangre*, etc. On the other hand, new neuter formations of this type (*lens-dis* > **lenden-ine* > OIt. *lendine*. Sard. *lendiri*, Sic. *lénninu*, Sp. *liendre*; *circes-itis* > **circen-ine* > It. *cercine*, Friulan *čerčin*, Sp. *cercén*; *glans-dis* > **glanden-ine* > Sp. *landre* are cited by Ascoli and accepted by Meyer-Lübke. The implication of these new forms works havoc with the theory that imparisyllabic neuter forms and the sense of the neuter gender vanished at an early period, and in consequence casts an unfavorable light upon the assumption that many such neuters were absorbed by the masculine gender and developed into Romance from the new accusative form.

III. 2. b. *'-men, '-mine.*

1. Preceded by a consonant: *cármen, cúlmen, frágmen, fúlmen, gérmen, *ólmen, *púlmen, ségmen, tégmen, térmen, *vérmen*—Fr. *charme*, apparently an ablative survival, is claimed by Körting to have been reconstructed from the verb *charmer*; It. *carme, carmine*, though not advanced by either side, present interesting possibilities. Roum. *culme*, It. *colmo*, Piedmontese *korme*, Engadine *kuolm* appear to be accusative survivals; OF *coume*, MF *comble* are noncommittal, while Sp. *cumbre*, despite its crossing with *cumulus*, seems to belong to the ablative group, as also Cadorino *cólmen*; It. *culmine* is rejected by Meyer-Lübke as learned. It. *frana* and Roum. *fărămă* appear to be derived from the plural *fragmina*. It. *fulmine*, from the ablative, rejected by Meyer-Lübke as a learned word, is defended by Ascoli on the ground of derivation from *fŭlgmen* > *fŭlmen*; while, on the one hand, learned origin for a word of this type appears far-fetched, added proof of its popular origin and use may be found in Sic. *fúrgini*, a cross between **fulgere* (< *fulgure*) and *fulmine*, obviously in the ablative. It. *germe* and Prov. *germ* being conceded as accusative survivals, Fr. *germe*, It. *germine* and Sp. *germen* are discarded as learned by Meyer-Lübke, while Ascoli claims for It. a double series *germe, germine, addome, addomine, vime, vimine*, and scoffs at the idea of so many nouns in everyday use being claimed as learned. Roum. *olmu* and Pt. *polme*, from the two hypothetical forms in our list, appear to favor the accusative

(but for *polme,* as well as Pt. *cume* < *culmen* and all other Pt. forms of this type, see below under *-men* preceded by a stressed vowel). The derivation of Sp. *sien* from the acc. *segmen* is doubtful, a more likely derivation being the Germanic *sin*.[20] The accusative *tegmen* has its descendants in Ferrara *tiem,* Como *tem* and Ven. *tiemo,* while Prov. *teume* favors the ablative. *Termen* has as its descendants Roum. *term,* Genoese and Luccan *terme,* Engadine *tierm* and Tyrolese *termo,* while *termine* is followed by It. *termine,* Sic. *termini,* Calabr. *tiermine,* Neap. *termənə,* Bologna *termen,* Friulan *tiermi,* Fr. Prov., Cat. *terme*; and the hypothetical form *termite by Neap. *termə,* Friulan *tiarmit,* Fr. *tertre,* Freiburg *tyerdu* and Walloon *tyern*; doubt attaches to the Roum. feminine *termure,* while Meyer-Lübke, who claims derivation from *terminus* for the French and Friulan forms, has no explanation for the It. literary and dialectal forms save the somewhat unsatisfactory one that they represent a cross between *termen* and *terminus.* Tuscan *vermine,* Milan. *vermen,* Abbruz. *vermənə,* Romagna *vírman,* Bearn, *bermi,* Prov., Cat. *verme,* OSp. *biermen, bierven,* OPt. *vermen,* side by side with It. *verme,* Bergamo *vérem, vérom,* Log. *berme, merme,* Campid. *gremi,* Engad. *verm,* Friulan *vierm,* Fr. *ver,* Prov., Cat. *verm,* Sp., Pt. *verme* are claimed by both Ascoli and Meyer-Lübke as evidence of the passage of *vermis* to *vermen. Here again the implication is in favor of a long-lived neuter gender for nouns of this type, strong enough in Vulgar Latin times to attract masculines and, as a corollary, to resist the attraction claimed by many writers in the case of nouns of this type.

2. Preceded by an unstressed vowel: **líquimen, pérgamen,* **regálimen, régimen*—These four forms, the only ones that show accent-shift among *-men* nouns, are relatively unimportant. Milan. *lem* < acc. *liquimen is considered doubtful by Meyer-Lübke. Prov. *pergan, pargan* presents obvious difficulties, both from the accusative and from the ablative standpoints, and Meyer-Lübke is probably justified in calling it a back-formation. Fr. *royaume,* Prov. *reyalme* and OSp. *realme, reame* < *regalimen favor the accusative, while OF *reemme, reame* seems to be from the ablative *regimine*; It. *regimine,* Prov. *regime* and MF *régime* are rejected by

---

[20] *Diccionario de la Real Academia, s. v.*

Meyer-Lübke as learned forms. Of some interest among these forms is OSp. *realme,* which Meyer-Lübke and Baist [21] claim is a loanword from French; if we reject this hypothesis, which is not advanced by Diez (and there is nothing in the phonetic development of the word to prove that it is not native to Spain), we have a clear-cut case of accusative derivation in a noun of a type for which Spanish ordinarily prefers the ablative development.

3. *-men* nouns with a stressed vowel preceding being over 50 in number, it will be best to take them individually. Generally speaking, they give *-me* in It., Roum. and Pt., *-m* in Fr., Prov. and Rhetian, *-mbre* in Sp., *-men, -mene, -mine* in Log. The It., Roum., Fr., Prov. and Rhetian forms are generally conceded as accusative. Conflict arises over the Sp. and Log. forms (see pp. 35-39). As for the Pt., which is conceded, even by Ascoli, to be of accusative origin, certain considerations present themselves which have not been previously advanced.

The double forms of Logudorese (*-men, -mene* or *-mine*; in Campidanese only *-mine, -mini*), advanced by Ascoli as definite proof of double derivation, are rejected by Meyer-Lübke and his supporters on the ground that the longer forms simply represent an accusative *-men* with the addition of epenthetic *-e*. To this assumption many objections arise. In the first place, a dialect which is capable of regularly preserving an *-n* ending in nouns and elsewhere might find epenthetic *-e* superfluous; or, if it made use of it, might be expected to extend it universally. Secondly, considering the conservatism of Logudorese in the matter of vowels, both stressed and unstressed, we might expect to find *-mene,* but not *-mine,* if Meyer-Lübke's theory held true; [22] on the contrary, *-mine* forms predominate in Logudorese (*-mine, -mini* is exclusively used in Campidanese, but the vocalism of this dialect shows frequent changes of *e* to *i*). Furthermore, Ascoli presents from an older work [23] a double series in nouns of this type, from which it appears that the

---

[21] *Romanische Forschungen,* XIX, 639.

[22] For the controversy on this important point, cf. Meyer-Lübke, *Zur Kenntniss der Altlogudoresischen,* and F. Mohl. *Lexique du latin vulgaire,* 26; the latter holds that *-mene* forms are analogical, and that the conflict between *-men* and *-mine* is indicative of a real struggle for supremacy between the oblique cases.

[23] Spano, *Ortografia sarda,* I, 57.

two forms were once used in accordance with their function (*su nomen, su samben, su semen* in the nominative and accusative, but *de su nomene, de su sambene*, etc., after prepositions). This point, which Meyer-Lübke leaves unexplained, would tend to show that Log. preserved not only the double form, but even the double function in nouns of this type. Lastly, Ascoli, in refuting the epenthetic vowel theory for Italian (the refutation applies equally well to Sardinian), points out that such additions are never reflected in the masculine system, where we might reasonably expect, from the nominative, such forms as **pátere, *mégliore*, side by side with *suoro, uomo, ladro, nievo*, etc., had the tendency to add epenthetic *-e* been so widespread. It would seem, therefore, that we must take Meyer-Lübke's exception to Ascoli's classification with a considerable dose of skepticism.

In connection with Sp. *-mbre*, which is apparently the phonetical descendant of *-mine* rather than of *-men*, it is of some interest to note the divergent opinions of those who hold to the pure accusative theory. Menéndez-Pidal [24] and Hanssen [25] hold that these nouns were treated as masculines (*vimen > *viminem > mimbre*). Grandgent [26] holds the same theory (**nominem*), though elsewhere [27] he claims that *-n* was generally dropped save in monosyllabic words (**nome*). Bourciez [28] offers the following development: *nomen, lumen > *nomine, *lumine > nombre, lumbre*. Diez [29] holds that *-mbre* comes from *-men* through the intermediate stages *-m'n, -mne*. This view is accepted by Nyrop. [30] Meyer-Lübke shows some hesitation in his statements; in the morphological section of his work [31] he seems to accept Diez's view, at least by implication (*-men > -mbre*); in the phonetic part [32] he gives the following development: *m'n >* Sp. *mr, mbr*, and adds: "The same change of *-ne* to *-re* occurs in the case of a group composed of *n* + consonant + *ne* (*sanguine > sangre*)."

---

[24] *Manual de gramática histórica española*, pp. 180-182.
[25] *Gramática histórica de la lengua castellana*, 167.
[26] *Introd. to V. L.*, 347.
[27] *Ibid.*, 310.
[28] *Eléments de linguistique romane*, 218c.
[29] *Grammatik der romanischen Sprachen*, II, 2-7.
[30] *Op. cit.*, II, 229.
[31] *Op. cit.*, II, 11.
[32] *Op. cit.*, I, 526.

Ascoli, assuming the obvious phonetic development *-mine* > *-m'ne* > **mre* > *-mbre*, as in *homine(m)* > *hombre*, also takes care to point out certain rare cases in which Spanish chose the accusative form, with a widely divergent phonetic outcome (*bitumen* > *betún, lignamen* > *leñame, sagimen* > *saín*). To his examples, we may add *letame* < *laetamen* and possibly *realme* < **regalimen*, even without making use of the *crimen* and *flumen* which Meyer-Lübke calls learned. Ascoli further points to OSp. *nome*, side by side with *nomne* and *nombre*, as proof of double derivation, and is borne out by Körting, who gives the forms *nom, non* for OSp.

In reply to the views of Menéndez-Pidal, Hanssen and Grandgent, the point may be made that the fluctuation between masculine and neuter forms, working, as we have seen, both ways (*lens* > **lenden, vermis* > **vermen*, etc.), is an unsatisfactory explanation; that the loss of the neuter gender for nouns did not occur till early Romance times;[33] and that consequently the question remains open why or how in certain sections a neuter form should have survived (*nomen* > It. *nome*) and in others have been supplanted by a hypothetical masculine (**nominem* > Sp. *nombre*); (Hanssen, indeed, claims that while in Spanish these nouns became masculine, in Portuguese they remained neuter). The question also remains open why, if we grant a wholesale shift from the neuter to the masculine, eliminating conflict between the two neuter forms, such words as *bitumen, laetamen, lignamen* and *sagimen* should not have been submerged by the general tendency and have developed into **bedumbre, *ledambre, *leñambre* and **saímbre*.

Bourciez's views are, to say the least, strange. Why assume new long forms **nomine* and **lumine* when these forms were already in existence and at the disposal of Vulgar Latin speakers in Spain?

Lastly, the theory of Diez and Nyrop is untenable on historical as well as phonetic grounds. Probable disappearance of Classical Latin final *-n* is indicated in Vulgar Latin,[34] so that *nomen* would become **nome* before it could turn into **nom'n*. But. even if this were not so, just how could *nomen* turn phonetically into **nom'n*, the necessary prerequisite for **nom'ne*? In view of the fact that

---

[33] Grandgent, *Introd. to V. L.*, 349.
[34] Bourciez, *op. cit.*, 55; but cf. also Grandgent, *Introd. to V. L.*, 310.

Spanish regularly admits of a *-men* ending in verbs (*lamen, comen, imprimen, consumen*), why should the necessity of changing *famen, nomen, vimen, lumen* into such unpronounceable combinations as *fam'n, nom'n, vim'n, lum'n* have been felt? Guarnerio,[35] a specialist in phonology, logically derives all Spanish forms in *-mbre* from *-mine*, and masculine nouns of the type of *hombre* bear out this view.

In connection with Portuguese forms in *-me*, which the accusative forces claim for and Ascoli concedes to the accusative, an investigation of Pt. phonology brings to light some interesting facts. The development of the *m'n* group in Pt., as well as of nouns of the *-men* type, is carefully avoided by most historical grammarians, including Meyer-Lübke himself.[36] Nunes,[37] to cite another instance, speaking of *m'n* says: "êle se não formou en *vime* ou *vimen* (arc.), *ome* (arc. e pop.) ou *homem, costume, semear*, etc.", and goes no further, save to inform us that wherever *m'n* > *mbr*, this is due to Spanish influence.

Cornu, in Gröber's *Grundriss*,[38] speaks of original *mn* > *n* (*outono, dano, escano*). But this, or a similar development (*m'n* > *m*) also appears to apply to *m'n* brought about by syncopation (*domino* > *dom'no* > *dono; termino* > *term'no* > *termo; homine* > *hom'ne* > *ome*). It is worthy of note, in this connection, that both Meyer-Lübke and Körting derive Pt. *fome* from **faminen* or **famine*, not from *famen*. May we therefore not be justified in assuming that Pt. *lume* may be the descendant of *lumine* (with syncopation and progressive assimilation) rather than of *lumen*, particularly since we find in Pt. such exceptional forms as *sem* < *semen* and possibly *farum, farun* < **ferumen*, which stand to the regular development in the same ratio as Sp. *betún, leñame*, etc., to the customary Sp. *-mbre*?

All in all, therefore, it would appear that Logudorese, Spanish and possibly Portuguese favor the ablative development in nouns of this type to the same extent to which Italian, Roumanian, French, Provençal and Rhetian favor the accusative. The notable exceptions

---

[35] *Op. cit.*, pp. 484-485.
[36] *Op. cit.*, I, 526.
[37] *Compendio de gramática histórica portuguesa*, 137.
[38] *Grundriss der romanischen Philologie*, I, 968.

ACCUSATIVE OR OBLIQUE? 41

which we meet in each and every language group, as we shall see below, are simply evidence of the conflict that took place over the entire Romance area at the point when a choice became imperative.

* * *

acímen—Prov. *azim, from which the verb *azimá* is derived, would be of accusative origin.

acrúmen—It. *agrume,* Sic. *agrumi,* OF *aigrum,* MF *aigrain, égrain,* MProv. *eigrüm,* are all accusative survivals.

acúmen—Pt. *gume,* the only sure form, may be of ablative origin.

aerámen—Roum. *aramă,* It. *rame,* North Sard. *ramu,* Engad. *aram,* Obwald. *irom,* OF *arain,* MF *airain,* Prov., Cat. *aram* are from the accusative; Log. *ramine,* Campid. *arromini,* Sp. *arambre, alambre* and perhaps Pt. *arame* from the ablative.

albúmen—Roum. *albime,* It. *albume* are from the accusative; It. *albumine* (learned?) from the ablative.

*allevámen, *allevímen*—It. *allevime,* Piacenza, Parma *alvam,* OF *alevain, alevin,* Cat. *aleví,* Morvan *alvẽ,* Pt. (Beira) *alabão, alavão* are from the accusative.

alúmen—It. *allume,* Fr. *alun,* Prov. *alum* < acc.; Sp. *alumbre,* perhaps Pt. (*pedra*) *hume* < abl.

arcámen—It. *arcame, carcame* < acc.

bitúmen—It. *bitume,* Fr. *betun, béton,* Prov., Cat. *betun,* Sp. *betún* < acc.

caldúmen—It. *caldume,* Sic. *quadumi,* Bologna *kaldom,* OVen. *kaldume,* Piazza Armerina *kaudum,* OF *chaudun,* MF *chaudin,* West Fr. *šodẽ,* Majorca *eskaldom* < acc.

consuetúmen—It. *costume,* Log. *costumen* < acc.; Log. *costumene,* OSp. *costumne,* MSp. *costumbre,* perhaps Pt. *costume* < abl. Fr. *coutume,* Prov. *cosdumna* probably < plural *costumina.* In connection with Sp. forms in *-mbre,* Ascoli, forestalling the contention that they may come from the plural, takes care to point out that they are by no means universally feminine (*alambre, enjambre, mimbre, nombre, pelambre,* etc.).

coriámen—It. *corame,* Log. *koramen,* Engad. *küram,* Friulan *koream,* OF *curien* < acc.; Sp. *corambre,* perhaps Pt. *corame* < abl.

crímen—OIt. *crime,* Prov. *crim,* Sp. *crimen* < acc. It *crimine,* Fr.

crime, possibly Pt. *crime* < abl. (the It., Su. and Fr. forms are disputed by Meyer-Lübke as learned).

discrímen—Sic., Abbruz. *skrima* appear to be from the plural.

exámen—It. *sciame, sciamo*, Log. *esamen*, Fr. *essaim*, Prov. *eisam*, Cat. *eixam* < acc.; Log. *esaminu*, Sp. *enjambre*, possibly Pt. *enxame* < abl. Obwald. *šaum*, Engadine *sem*, in view of their different development from the more common *-om*, *-am* for nouns of this type (Obw. *irom, curom*, Engad. *aram, cüram*) are attributed by Ascoli to *examine*. Meyer-Lübke denies this, and derives these exceptional forms from verbs or from the plural, accounting in the same way for the double Bergamo form *samen, sam*; his demonstration is admittedly hypothetical.

*fámen (< *fames*)— While the shorter forms (Roum. *foame*, It. *fame*, Fr. *faim*, OSp. *fame*, etc.) may be ascribed to *fames*, Log. *famen* is from the acc. *famen, and Log. *famine*, Campid. *famini*, Gascon *hami*, Sp. *hambre* and possibly Pt. *fome* from the abl. *famine.

farcímen—OF *farcin* < acc.

ferrúmen—Sp. *herrumbre* < abl.

*ferúmen—Cat. *farum*, Pt. *farum, farun* possibly < acc.

flúmen—It. *fiume*, Log. *flumen*, OF, Prov., Rhetian *flum* < acc.; Log. *flumine* < abl.

forámen—It. *forame* < acc.; Sp. *horambre*, possibly Pt. *forame* < abl.

*frigidámen—Pt. *friame, freame* possibly < abl.

frúmen—OF *enfrum*, Prov. *enfrun* < acc.

*funámen—Fr. *funin*, Prov. *funam* < acc.

grámen—Log. *ramen*, Trento *agram*, Prov. *gram* < acc.; Sp., Pt. *grama* < plural.

*incisámen—OGenoese *inzisame*, Cat. *enciam* < acc.

laetámen—Veglia *lotum*, It. *letame*, Abruz., Lucca *lutame*, Ven. *leame, loame*, Lomb. *ledam*, Milan, *aldam*, Brianza, Vaudois *leam*, Sp. *letame* < acc.; possibility of abl. or double origin appears in Neap. *lotamme*, Monferrato *aliám, aliame*, Gen. *liame, liamme*, Molfetta *remete*, Bari *remmate*, Tarent. *rummato*, while Log. *ledamine* < abl.

legúmen—Roum. *legumă*, It. *legume*, Brescia *lim*, Friulan *liums*, OF *leun*, Prov. *leum*, Cat. *llegum* < acc.; Log. *legumene*, Sp. *legumbre*, possibly Pt. *legume* < abl. Walloon *éume*, Piedmont, Monferrato *ləmu*, Vaudois *lömene*, Lomb., Gen., Emilian *leme*, are admitted by Meyer-Lübke to be exceptional forms, for which no explanation is offered. The Walloon and Vaudois forms present very definite ablative possibilities.

levámen—OVen. *levame*, Obwald, *levont*, Friulan *levam*, Fr. *levain*, Prov. *levan* < acc.

ligámen—It. *legame*, Abruz. *ləhamə*, Log. *ligamen*, Engad. *liam*, Friulan *leamb*, Fr. *lien*, Savoy *lẽ*, Prov. *liam* > acc.

lignámen—It. *legname*, Prov. *lenham*, Cat. *llenyam*, Sp. *leñame* < acc.; Log. *linnamine* < abl. (Meyer-Lübke claims that the Sp. form is derived from It., but the evidence for this is not clear; if it were, should not the same derivation also apply to *letame*, which appears in Old Spanish?)

límen—Engad. *im*, *lims*, Tyrol. *lim* < acc.; Como *limni* appears to be a plural form, though abl. derivation is possible.

*lorámen—OF *lorain* < acc.

lúmen—Roum. *lume*, It. *lume*, Bologna *lom*, Lomb. *lüm*, Prov. *lum*, Cat. *llum* < acc.; It. *lumine*, Log. *lumene*, Poschiavo *lumen*, Sp. *lumbre*, possibly Pt. *lume*, OProv. *lume*, Dauphiné, Vaudois *lüme* < abl. Speaking of these last two forms, Meyer-Lübke says that they agree with Spanish, but suppose development from *-mne*.

*materiámen—OF *merrien*, MF *merrain*, Prov. *mairam* < acc.

medicámen—OSp. *meegambre*, MSp. *vedegambre* < abl.

nómen—Roum. *nume*, Veglia *nam*, It. *nome*, Log. *nomen*, Engad., Friul., Fr., Prov., Cat. *nom*, OSp. *nome*, *nom*, *non* < acc.; Log. *lumene*, Campid. *nomini*, Gascon *numi*, OSp. *nomne*, MSp. *nombre*, perhaps Pt. *nome* < abl. Ascoli cites from Burguy an OF form *noune*, also given by Webster as one of the possible derivations of the English *noun*, which, with *nom*, shows a possible double development in French.

nutrímen—Trento *lodrin*, Engad. *nudrim*, Friulan *nudrum*, Morvan *nõre*, Prov. *noirim* < acc.

*ossámen—Roum. *osime*, It. *ossame* < acc.

*pellámen—It. *pellame*, Fr. *plain*, Prov. *pelam*, Cat. *pellam* < acc.; Log. *peddamine*, Sp. *pelambre*, possibly Pt. *pellame* < abl.

*pilámen—It. *pelame*, Friulan *pelam*, Fr. *pelin*, Prov. *pelam* < acc.; Sp. *pelambre*, possibly Pt. *pelame* < abl. (Note that for the Sp. form there seems to be confusion between *pellamen and *pilamen.)

*putrímen—Fr. *purin* < acc.

*sagímen—It. *saíme*, Piedmont *sim*, OF *saïn, saim*, MF *sain(-doux)*, Prov. *sagin, saïn*, Cat. *sagin, sagi*, Sp. *saín* < acc. (The derivation *sagimen is given by Diez and Körting; Meyer-Lübke prefers *saginum*, and explains the It. form as derived from OF and the Sp. from Prov. or OF;[39] but in this he is contradicted by Gröber,[40] who claims that the Sp. form is native to Spain and corresponds to a regular Spanish phonetic development from the acc. *sagimen. The *Diccionario de la Real Academia* derives Sp. *saín* from *sagina*, with little regard for gender or phonetic development.)

*salámen—It. *salame* is probably a late formation.

*sedímen (< *sédĭmen*)—OIt. *sedime*, Canavese *sim*, Friulan *sedim* < acc.

sémen—It. *seme*, Log. *semen*, Pt. *sem* < acc.; Log. *semene*, Campid. *semini* < abl.

stámen—It. *stame*, Log. *istamen*, Engad. *stom*, Fr. *étaim*, Prov., Cat. *estam* < acc.; Log. *istamine*, Sp. *estambre*, possibly Pt. *estame* < abl.

strámen—It. *strame*, Engad. Friulan *stram*, Fr. *étrein*, Prov. *estram* < acc.; Log. *istramine*, possibly Lecce *šome*, Pt. *estrume* < abl. The "striking vowel-change" of which Meyer-Lübke speaks in connection with the Pt. and Lecce forms may be of the same nature as that of Pt. *fome* < *famine, which he and Körting seem to attribute by implication to the influence of the *m'n* group rather than of the initial labial.

súmen—Log. *sumen, sumene* shows both developments. The "Sardinian" form *sume* given by Körting is remarkable in that it has dropped the final *-n*, unless it comes from the north of the island, where an Italian development would be possible.

vegetámen—Sp. *vegedambre*, offered by Körting, is not listed by the *Diccionario de la Real Academia*.

vímen—OIt. *vime* < acc.; It. *vimine*, Abbruz. *vimələ, vimbrə*, OF *vime*, Prov., Cat. *vime*, Sp. *vimbre, mimbre*, possibly Miranda *brime*, Pt. *vime* < abl. Other forms (Bologna *vemna*, Treviso *límana*, Asturian *blimba*, Galician *minvia* < plural).

---

[39] *Literaturblatt für germ. u. rom. Philologie*, XII, 302.
[40] *Archiv für lat. Lexicographie*, V, 456.

viridúmen—It. *verdume*, OF *verdum* < acc.; Log. *birdumen, birdumine* shows both developments.

volúmen—It. *vilume*, Sic. *mmurmu, mulmu*, Calabr. *mburmu* < acc.; Sp. *balum(b)a* < plural; Fr. *volume* probably learned.

In conclusion, the study of *-men* forms indicates a preference for the acc. in Roum., It., Rhetian, Fr. and Prov. territory, and for the abl. in Sp. and possibly Pt., with double development in Sard., and enough forms running counter to the general trend in every area except Roumania to give definite evidence of conflict (Sic. *termini, furgini*; Abruz. *vimele, vimbrə*; Rhet. *cólmen, lumen*; OF *noune, vime*; Prov. *teume, lume*; Vaudois *lömene, lüme*; Gascon *hami, numi*; OSp. *nome, nom, letame, saín*; Pt. *sem, farum*).

* * *

III. 3. *'-er, '-ere*.

ácer, cadáver, cícer, papáver, píper, súber, túber (túfer), úber, zíngiber—For this group, absorption by the masculine is claimed by some proponents of the accusative theory;[41] this question of absorption, already partly discussed in connection with *-men* nouns, will be again taken up later. Disregarding for the moment the possibility of **cicerem, *uberem*, etc., we have the following developments:

Roum. *artar*, Pt. *acer* seem to favor the acc.; It. *acero*, Lomb. *agre*, Trieste *aire*, Sp. *azre, arce* the abl.; while other North Italian forms, as well as Fr. *érable*, Prov. *izerablo*, Cat. *ars*, are non-committal. Calabr. *katafaru*, favors the abl., while Ascoli reports from Spano's work a double form *su cadaver, de su cadavere* for Logudorese. It. *cece*, Campobasso *čečə*, Bologna *tseis*, MF *(pois) chiche*, Prov. *cezer*, Asturian *chichu* favor accusative derivation (with some doubt for the Prov. form). while Macedo-Roum. *teatire*, Neapol. *čečerə*, Tarent. *čičiri*, Sic. *čičiru, kerkiri*, Campid. *čižiri* and possibly OF *ceire, çoire* and Sp., Pt. *chícharo* favor the ablative. Rhetian *pavar, pave*, Irpino *papañ* may favor the accusative, while It. *papavero, papavere*, OVen. *pavero* Abruz. *papambələ*, Neap. *frapavələ*

---

[41] Meyer-Lübke, *op. cit.*, II, 14; Grandgent, *Introd. to V. L.*, 347; Menéndez-Pidal, *op. cit.*, 180-182.

and Log. *pabaúle* favor the ablative derivation; North Italian, Spanish and Portuguese forms are too corrupt to be of value (in connection with this word, it must be stated that the masc. *papaverem* appears in Plautus). It *pepe* comes from the acc., OIt. *pevere,* Veglia *pepro,* Log. *pibere,* Sp. *pebre* from the abl., while the Rhetian, French, Provençal and Catalan forms are non-committal, and Roum. *piper* appears to be a Greek or Slavonic loan-word. It. *sovero, sughero,* Log. *súaru,* Prov. *sieure* and Pt. *sovro* appear to favor the abl., while North Italian and Rhetian forms are of doubtful derivation. It. *(tar) tufo* and possibly Rhetian *(tar) tuffel* favor the acc., while North It., Fr., Prov. and Cat. forms are derived from the plural. Roum. *uger,* though crossed with *suge,* is apparently from the acc., while Macedo-Roum. *udzîre,* OIt. *uvero,* Friulan *l'uvri* and Sp., Pt. *ubre* favor the abl.; the contrast between Friulan *l'uvri* and Engadine *uver* is of interest as showing possible double development. *Zingiber,* which more often occurs in the indeclinable form *zingiberi,* suffers from the disadvantage of being an obviously foreign word; yet Italian, with its many forms (*zénzero, zénzavo, zénzamo* and *zenzóvero, zenzávero, gengióvo*) appears to offer both developments; Roum. *ghimber* favors the acc., while Fr. *gingembre,* Prov., Cat. *gingebre,* Sp. *gengibre,* Pt. *gengivre* are either from the abl. or from the indeclinable form.

Of particular interest in this group are the double developments. If we grant the contention that nouns of this class passed from the neuter to the masculine gender, how can we account for the many neuter accusative forms still in existence, and still more, for the double developments within the same language? If *piper* had become *piperem and *cicer* **cicerem,* we could account for It. *pevere* and Neap. *čečərə,* but not for *pepe* and *cece.* How can we contrast the development of Macedo-Roum. *udzîre* and *teatire* against Moldavo-Wallachian *uger* and *ghimber,* or of Prov. *cezer* against *sieure*? In this class, it would seem, the outcome of the conflict was less decisive than anywhere else in the neuter field.

* * *

III. 4. *'-or, '-ore*.

mármor—It. *marmo* and possibly Sp. *mármol* are from the acc.; It. *marmore,* Grado *nalbare,* Log. *marmaru,* Campid. *marmori* are from the abl.; Rhetian, French, Prov. and Cat. forms are non-committal, while Roum. *marmure, marmoră* and Neap. *marmola* may, as Meyer-Lübke suggests, come from **petra marmora* or from the plural (the masculine *marmorem* appears in Pliny).

* * *

III. 5. a. *'-ur, '-ore*.

fémur, róbur—Obwald. *famau* is of doubtful derivation. It. *rovere*, Campid. *orroli*, Prov., Cat. *roure*, Sp., Pt. *roble* appear to come from the abl.; Fr. *rouvre* is non-committal; note the possible double development in Engad. *luvar*, Poschiavo *rúal*, vs. Friulan *rori*.

* * *

III. 5. b. *'-ur, '-ure*.

fúlgur, gúttur, *mámphur, súlfur, (súlpur)—Roum. *fulger*, Friulan *folg* < acc.; It. *folgore*, OAbruz. *folgiore*, MAbruz. *frovələ*, Neap. *fruvolə*, Tarent. *fruvolo*, Sic. *furgaru, fúaru* < abl.; Fr. *fuildre, foldre, foudre* are non-committal, but note the possible double derivation in Prov. *folzer, foldre*. ONeap. *gutture*, Sic., Log. *gutturu* appear to favor the abl.; Obwald. *guotter*, Fr. *goître*, Vaudois *guitre* are non-committal; (note that a masculine *gutturem* occurs in Plautus). The form **mamphur*, with its Oscan branch **manfar* and its Latin **mandar* is of doubtful gender; Sienese *manfa* as opposed to *manfano, manfero*, Urbino *manfre*, and Campid. *maffu* vs. *maffulu* may indicate double development. Macedo-Roum. *sclifur*, It. *zolfo*, Tarent. *zurfo* < acc., while It. *solforo*, Log. *sulfuru*, Sp. *azufre*, Pt. *enxofre* < abl., with doubtful Rhetian, Fr., Prov. and Cat. forms.

In conclusion, nouns of the *'-or, '-ur* type indicate at least as many ablative as accusative derivations in the languages where a phonetic distinction con be made. Furthermore, doble developments in the same language (It. *marmo, marmore, zolfo, solforo*) afford a good refutation of the claim that these nouns passed into the masculine gender, in spite of their sporadic appearances as masculines in Latin authors. Note also the different development in the same language of nouns of similar types (Macedo-Roum. *teatire, udzîre* < *cicere, ubere* vs. *sclifur* < *sulfur*).

III. 6. a. *'-us, '-ere*.

ácus, génus, glómus, látus, ónus, ópus, póndus, rúdus, sídus, véllus, vúlnus—Abruz. *ačərə* is from the ablative. Roman *geno*, OF *giens*, Prov. *ge(n)s* < acc.; It. *genere*, Fr., Prov. *genre*, Sp., Pt. *género* < abl.; the claim that the latter forms are learned, made by Körting, Grandgent and others, is admitted by Ascoli for Sp. and Pt., but denied for It., Fr. and Provençal. Roum. *ghem*, It. *ghiomo*, Luccan *diomo*, Ven. *ǧemo*, Mantuan *ǧemb*, Trento *ǧomo*, OProv. *gloms* are from the acc., while It. gnomero, Neap. l'uómmərə, Tarent. *ñuémmiru*, Calabr. *gyómbiru*, Sic. *gyómmaru*, Log. *lórurnu*, Campid. *lómburu* seem to be of ablative derivation; Meyer-Lübke, in connection with the latter forms, states that the south of Italy prefers *gnomer-*, while Nigra [42] derives them from a form **glomŭru*, derived in turn from *glomere* It. *lato*, Veglia *(a)liť*, OLog. *ladus*, Friulan *lai*, OF *lez*, Prov. *latz*, Sp., Pt. *lado* are from the accusative; the only ablative form is Roum. *lature*; but this is claimed by Nyrop and Meyer-Lübke to be reconstructed from the plural. Log. *onus* comes from the acc., while It. *onere* is probably learned. Roum. *op (este), opt*, It. *uopo*, Log. *obus*, OF *ues*, Prov., Cat. *ops*, OSp. *huebos* are of accusative origin; Ascoli claims that Fr. masculine *œuvre* is a descendant of the ablative *opere*, and is supported in this by Littré. Sic. *punna* and Cat. *(a) pons* come from the acc. *pondus*. Emilian *rud* and Lombard *rüd* come from the accusative; but It. *rudere*, defended as a popular word by Ascoli on the ground of popular derivation in Sp. *rudéra* < **rudaria*, and Friulan *rudine*, appears to be of ablative origin. OIt. *sido* comes from the accusative. It. *vello*, Log. *biddu(s)*, Prov. *vel*, Sp., Pt. *vello* are of accusative origin, but OF *velre, viaure* come from the ablative. Pt. *vurmo, burmo, brumo*, apparently from the acc., and Fr. *gourme, bourme* are of doubtful derivation. To this class, Ascoli adds *ulcus* and *viscus*, claiming It. *ulcere* and *viscere* as direct ablative descendants rather than learned forms, as alleged by Meyer-Lübke. Ascoli's discussion of the possibility of long *u* in *ulcus* (< IE *Felkos, Folkos*) is of interest.

* * *

---

[42] *Archivio Glottologico*, XV, 490.

III. 6. b. '-us, '-ore.

*ácus, córpus, *fémus, frígus, *fúndus, litus, péctus, pécus, pígnus, stércus, témpus—Roum. ac, It. ago, Abruz. akə, Log. agu, Veglia yuak could be construed as acc. derivatives were it not for the possibility of a direct passage from the feminine acus-ūs to the masculine; the only form that justifies a neuter *acus is the plural It. agora. Roum. corp, It. corpo, Log. corpus, Engad. küerp, Friulan kuarp, Fr. corps, Prov. cors, Cat. cos, Sp. cuerpo, Pt. corpo all come from the acc.; while for this noun the triumph of the acc. seems complete, and is reported at an early period,[43] note the curious double loan-word of Welsh, corff, corffor, reported by Ascoli as evidence of conflict. OF fiens, Prov. femps, Cat. fems are assumed by Meyer-Lübke to come from *fimus-oris rather than from the masc. fimus-i, with treatment similar to that of filius, puteus, etc. Roum. frig. South It. frigo, Campid. frius are from the accusative. Engad. fuonz, Friulan fonz, OF fonz, MF fonds, Prov. fons are assumed by Meyer-Lübke to be from *fundus-oris rather than from the masc. fundus-i, possibly on the evidence of Roum. plural funduri. It. lito and Ven. lido are from the accusative. Roum. piept, It. petto, Log. pettus, Engad. pech, Friulan pet, OF piz, Prov. peitz, OCat. pits, OSp. pechos, MSp. pecho, Pt. peito are from the acc.; Canavese, Dauphiné pitro, Savoy petre, Vaudois, Swiss Fr. petru, East Prov. pitre are from the ablative.[44] OUmbrian, Marche, Velletri peko, Log. pegus, Prov., Cat. pec, Pt. pego are from the acc., while Roum. pĕcure, fem. plural, appears to be a plural derivative. It. pegno, OLog. pinnus, Engad. pein, Friulan peñ, Prov. penh, OSp. peño come from the acc., while OVen. pegnora, Cat. pengora, Sp., Pt. prenda appear to come from the plural. ORoum. sterc, It. sterco, Sic. streu, Log. istercu, Asturian istiercu, Pt. esterco are of accusative origin, while Milan. stercol and Sp. estiércol come from the abl.; Meyer-Lübke's explanation of the Sp. form as derived from the verb estercolar is disputed by Ascoli on the analogy of mármol. Roum. timp, It. tempo, Log. tempus, Engad. temp, Friulan timp,

---

[43] Bechtel, S. Silviae Peregrinatio, 86 (corpo for corpore); but cf. note 55.
[44] Nigra, Archivio Glottologico, XV, 120, claims that these forms are derived from the "trisyllabic oblique of neuters in -us"; while Zauner, Rom. Forschungen, XIV, 476, though admitting that they come from pectore, calls them the result of a shift to the masculine declension.

Fr., Prov., Cat. *temps,* Sp. *tiempo,* Pt. *tempo* are of acc. origin; Roum. *timpla,* It. *tempia,* Log. *trempa,* etc., come from the plural; Obwald. *tumper* and OF *tempre(s)* are from the ablative; the value of these forms is not altogether destroyed by their adverbial use, while Friulan *templi* and OF and Prov. *temple,* [45] masculine singular, are difficult to explain as derived from *tempora.* Here again, Ascoli presents a Welsh loan-word doublet, *tymp, tymmor,* to prove the existence of a conflict.

While an accusative majority appears for nouns of the *'-us* type (which we may explain as due, at least in part, to a natural tendency on the part of such nouns to become confused with second declension masculines), the number and variety of ablative survivals in this class are so extensive as to refute the sweeping statements of accusative theorists like Meyer-Lübke and Nyrop. The claim that Italian nouns in this group are of learned derivation can hardly be advanced for *gnomero* or for such dialectal forms as Abbruz. *ać̌ərə.* The unanimity of Sardinian in favor of the accusative is broken by Log. *lórurnu,* Campid. *lómburu.* French, which was not in a position to contribute evidence in nouns of the *'-er, '-or, '-ur* type, enters this field with dialectal forms from *pectore,* and with *viaure, temple, œuvre* and an adverbial form, *tempre(s),* which is of as much value as the prepositional *lez* of the accusative proponents. The double form of Welsh loan-words from *corpus* and *tempus* would also seem to point to a definite conflict.

* * *

III. 7. *'-ut, '-ite.*

cáput—Roum. *cap,* Veglia *kup,* It. *capo, cavo,* Lomb. *ko,* Rhetian *k'af,* Log. *kabu,* Fr. *chef,* Prov., Cat. *cap,* Sp., Pt. *cabo* are derived from the acc. or from **capum-i.* Velletri *kapito,* Subbiaco *kapitu,* Milan. *kaved,* Log. *kabidu,* Campid. *kabide,* all of which appear to be of ablative derivation, are rejected by Meyer-Lübke as formations from the plural, along with Roum. *capet,* while Log.

---

[45] Zauner, *Rom. Forschungen,* XIV, 417, offers a masculine *temple* and a feminine *tempe* from the same region in Provence, but draws no conclusion.

kabude, Campid. *kabudu* are ascribed to *caput*, possibly with an epenthetic vowel.

* * *

As we have seen, proponents of the accusative theory have made use of every device to deny ablative derivations. Learned origin has been worked overtime; shifts of gender and declension, derivation from the plural and from verbs, epenthetic vowels, all have been called into play. In spite of this, certain forms, like OF *viaure*, Prov. *lume*, East Prov. *pitre*, defy explanation unless we derive them from the ablative.

The divergent opinions of the various accusative theorists may here again be referred to. While Menéndez-Pidal holds that *-r* and *-n* neuters became masculine, and derives *estiércol* from **stercore(m)*, Meyer-Lübke brings in the influx of the verb. While Meyer-Lübke and Nyrop derive such forms as *huebos* and *pecho(s)* from the accusative, Hanssen claims nominative influence for such forms, as well as for *cor* > *cuer*, and holds that while Sp. turned to the masculine for *enjambre*, Pt. retained the neuter in *enxame*. Bourciez[46] claims that the shift from the neuter to the masculine was an early phenomenon, but also asserts[47] that the change of *pulvis* to **pulvus-eris* shows long survival of neuter endings; while Grandgent[48] holds that the loss of the neuter gender for nouns was not complete till early Romance times, and Brunot[49] holds that the neuter was weakened but not lost by the sixth century. Grandgent's statement[50] that by the end of the Vulgar Latin period the cases generally retained were nominative and accusative-ablative (what we should call oblique), conflicts with his other statement[51] that in the singular the only surviving case is the accusative.

The wholesale shift of gender postulated by some writers is contradicted by several facts: both Meyer-Lübke and Grandgent[52]

---

[46] *Op. cit.*, 96a, 96b.
[47] *Op. cit.*, 218c.
[48] *Introd. to V. L.*, 349.
[49] *Histoire de la langue française*, 76-78.
[50] *Introd. to V. L.*, 354.
[51] *Ibid.*, 373.
[52] *Ibid.*, 347.

speak of the encroachment of neuter forms upon the masculines
(*cinus, *pulvus, etc.); such encroachments are far from showing a
weakening of neuter forms, at least for third declension imparisyllabic nouns. The continued survival and vast extension of -ora plurals [53] does not seem to indicate an early loss of neuter consciousness.

The value of such forms as *marmorem* in Pliny, *papaverem* in
Plautus, etc., has probably been overestimated. Such occurrences are
sporadic, and indicate a tendency, not an established state of affairs.
Occurrences of the type of *pectorem* in Gregory of Tours [54] (it was
pectus, not *pectore* or **pectorem*, that won out in western France);
corpo for *corpore* in the Peregrinatio Sylviae [55] (it was an *-us*, not
an *-o* form that won out in Old Spanish: *el Cuerpos Christi, dar
peños, hubo en tiempos*; *huebos, pechos,* etc.) [56] show that in a period of flux and conflict a form may appear and later vanish; but
this sporadic occurrence of such forms does indicate the existence
of a conflict.

The fact that an originally ablative form like *lumine* or *pipere*
may, at a time when final *-m* had long since vanished and syntactical
distinctions between accusative and ablative were confused, have
been seized upon and treated as an accusative (and this, after all,
is what some accusative theorists really imply when they postulate
**luminem* and **piperem*) need not greatly distress us. The fact that
should really concern us is that the ablative form has really survived, regardless of whatever remnants of gender or case-conscious-
ness may have been left in the minds of the speakers.

If we were to accept the theory of a wholesale shift of gender,
to what ought we to attribute the fact that this shift takes place
in some languages and not in others? And to what ought we to attribute cases of double development within the same language? If
pevere represents **piperem*, and *pepe* represents *piper*, are we to
suppose that a masculine and a neuter declension were continued
side by side, for the same word, in the same or contiguous territory?
Why was not this treatment extended to all imparisyllabic neuters,

---

[53] Bourciez, *op. cit.*, 218b, 428c, 484c; Grandgent, *Introd. to V. L.*, 369.
[54] Bonnet, *Le Latin de Grégoire de Tours*, 348.
[55] Bechtel, *op. cit.*, 86.
[56] Menéndez-Pidal, *op. cit.*, 180-182.

so that we might have in Romance the descendants of the masculine accusative *melle* instead of those of the neuter accusative *mel*?

In this connection, some additional evidence may be found in the development of a peculiar Latin adjective which had within itself the possibility of double development, and which synthesizes, so to speak, the entire situation. *Vetus* gives us It. *(Or)vieto*, OF *vies*, Lorrain *vyös*, while *vetere(m)* gives us It. *(Castel)vetro*, Sp. *(Mur)viedro*, Pt. *(Torres) Vedras*, as well as a variety of Italian, Rhetian and French dialectal forms (Bergamo *eder*, Engad. *veider*, Prov. *veiro*, etc.). If *vetus* had universally changed to *vetere(m)*, this change should be reflected in the former cases; if the point is made that *Orvieto* is a nominative, we ask why the same treatment was not extended to *Castelvetro*. It is quite evident that here, as in the imparisyllabic third declension neuters, there was a conflict of forms which could not phonetically coincide, and that this conflict was decided again by the triumph of the shorter form in certain cases, of the longer form in others.

All in all, the evidence is fairly clear that where accusative and ablative forms could not coincide, a conflict occurred which subsists to the present day, and this in each and every one of the fields cited by Meyer-Lübke and Nyrop: in monosyllabic words with (or without) final -*m*; in the sole Romance dialect where final -*o* and -*u* could be kept distinct; in the few dialects where umlaut of the root vowel is caused by the final vowel; and in imparisyllabic neuter nouns of the third declension. If the accusative seems to hold the upper hand in some sections of these fields, the fact need not disturb the defenders of the oblique case, for they are in a position to concede individual accusative survivals, whereas their opponents are under the necessity of disproving practically all ablative survivals in order to establish their claims.

If we now return for an instant to the evidence of the late Vulgar Latin texts, we find that the Tardif documents [57] present several interesting cases of *tempus, nomen* and *latus* used in the ablative function, in full harmony with later developments in northern France; we also find [58] several examples of *rem* in the ablative function,

---

[57] Pei, *op. .cit.*, 147.
[58] *Ibid.*, 152.

in accordance with subsequent *rien*. Cases similar to these have often been advanced by proponents of the accusative theory and used to demonstrate their beliefs. But if we accept the testimony of the texts for these cases, what justifies us in rejecting a far more voluminous mass of evidence from these same texts to the effect that *-a, -o, -e* were, in the eighth century, the predominant endings for all oblique case functions in northern France? The *whole* truth is, after all, part of the judicial formula, and those of us who have been philologically nurtured in an inductive study of the Vulgar Latin texts prefer accepting their complete testimony to following views that have been deductively established without reference to all of the available evidence.

The Romanic Review, XXVIII (1937)

IV

ACCUSATIVE VERSUS OBLIQUE IN PORTUGUESE

In the foregoing article, J. H. D. Allen, Jr. rejects the hypothesis that the development of neuter forms like *nomen, lumen,* etc. in Portuguese may point to ablative derivation, and claims, for words of this type, accusative derivation in accordance with the scheme *nomen* > *nome, lumen* > *lume,* etc., as opposed to *hominem* > *homine* > **homen* for masculine nouns with final *-e,* and *terminum* > *termio* > *termo* for nouns in which the final vowel is other than *-e.*

Despite the interesting discussion offered by the writer, several objections to his classification arise. Nunes, in the introduction to his *Chrestomathia archaica,* [1] claims the identical development for *homine* as for *termino* ("*terminu, termio, termo; homine, omee* e *ome*"), which is quite at variance with Allen's theory. Nunes also claims [2] that in *ome, sangue* and *costume* < *homine, sanguine* and **consuetumine,* the nasal resonance fell (*homine* > *omẽe* > *ome*); this, again, is at variance with Allen's claim that after the fall of the Latin final nasal, the resulting final *-e* also fell when preceded by *-n-,* thus leaving a new final nasal in Portuguese (*homine* > *omem* > *ome*).

In another work, [3] Nunes derives *lume* from "**lumine- (por lumen)*"; *arame* from "**eramine-*"; *víme* from "**vimine- (por vimen)*"; *gume* from "**acumine- (por acumen)*"; speaking of the fall

---

[1] Page lxxiv.
[2] Pages lxxv-lxxvi.
[3] *Compêndio de gramática histórica portuguesa,* p. 107.

of the nasal resonance,[4] he states that the forms which today appear as *verme, crime, gume, sangue, costume,* were formerly *vermẽ, *crimẽ, *gumẽ, *sanguẽ, *costumẽ*. It is of interest to note that while the phonetic process suggested by Nunes differs from either Allen's or mine, his derivations are from ablative, not accusative forms. Attention may also be called to the strident contradiction between Nunes' stand in the *Chrestomathia*,[5] where he derives *víme, lume* and other similar forms from *vimen, lumen,* etc., and the position he takes in the *Compêndio,* where he assumes, for precisely the same forms, derivation from *vimine, lumine,* etc. It is quite evident that confusion reigns in the mind of the Portuguese philologist in connection with nouns of this type; a confusion which, despite Allen's defense, is shared by Grandgent when he claims in one passage,[6] speaking of popular and late Latin, that "beside *lumen, nomen, piper* there must have been **luminem, *nominem, *piperem*"; and in another [7] that "the Romance languages" (not "some Romance languages") "indicate the disappearance of *-n* except in monosyllables; *nome(n), seme(n)*", etc. This confusion appears prevalent and, indeed, inevitable, among all those who refuse to accept the possibility of ablative derivation side by side with accusative development, and who are, in consequence, forced to sway back and forth, according to the forms that present themselves, from a phonetic derivation from the neuter accusative (*nomen* > *nome*) to a hypothetical transfer of gender (*vimen* > **viminem* > *vimem*).

A view totally different from either Allen's or Nunes' is taken by Antenor Nascentes in his *Dicionário etimológico da lingua portuguesa*; *s. v. costume,* which he derives, as does Nunes, from "**cosuetumine* en vez de *consuetudine*", he describes the process as follows: "Deu-se a síncope do ditongo protônico e a do *i* postônico. Depois no grupo *mn* o *n* se assimilou au *m* e o *m* dobrado simplificou-se." [8] This is precisely the development that I suggest for all nouns of this type in Portuguese.

---

[4] *Ibid.,* pp. 108-109.
[5] Page lxxv.
[6] *Introduction to Vulgar Latin,* § 347.
[7] *Ibid.,* § 310.
[8] "Syncopation of the pre-tonic diphthong and of the post-tonic *i* took place. Then, in the *mn* group, the *n* was assimilated to the *m,* and the doubled *m* was simplified."

It appears true that in the case of *nome* and *lume* no trace of the nasalization that characterizes *homem* appears in the early monuments of Portuguese. On the other hand, the form *vimem*, mentioned by Nunes in his *Compêndio*, [9] and appearing in the *Lusitania transformada* of Fernão Álvarez do Oriente, [10] is a clear-cut example of precisely such nasalization in the case of a neuter noun. If the development advanced by Allen for *homine* > *homem* is correct, then we cannot avoid the conclusion that *vimem* comes from *vimine* (this Nunes admits [11] when he places the development of *vimem* and *homem* in the same category); while if, in accordance with Allen's development, *vime* comes from *vimen*, we are faced with a splendid example of double development in Portuguese.

Lastly, it is to be noted that Allen derives *fome* from *famem*, unlike Meyer-Lübke and Körting, who favor derivation from **faminem* or **famine*, apparently on the basis of the unusual development of the stressed vowel; and that he offers no explanation of forms like *sem* < *semen* and *farun* < **ferumen*, cited by Körting, which, unless we assume them to be loan-words, seem to indicate a very unusual but unmistakable development from the accusative, with fall of the *-e* that becomes final, contrary to the general law laid down by Allen on the basis of his derivation of *nome* < *nomen* and *lume* < *lumen*.

In view of all these conflicting opinions and evidence, I believe I am still justified in asserting that there is a definite possibility that the Portuguese state of affairs favors derivations from the ablative.

The Romanic Review, XXX (1939)

---

[9] Page 127.
[10] "Com a fronte soberba sôbre o vimem", fl. 22 v.
[11] *Chrestomathia*, p. c.

V

LA COSTRUZIONE "IN CASA I FRESCOBALDI"

L'interessante problema sollevato dal Pasquali nel primo fascicolo di *Lingua Nostra* sembra ricollegarsi alla questione fondamentale della scomparsa del sistema morfologico del sostantivo latino, cui si sostituisce, ma solo gradatamente, il caso unico flessionale dell'italiano.

Già nell'ottavo secolo, prima dell'apparizione delle lingue neolatine, cominciano a delinearsi nei documenti notarili d'Italia e di Francia alcune tendenze che servono ad indicare l'evoluzione della lingua parlata. Mentre nei documenti francesi si stabilizza per la funzione del genitivo il tipo *Chramlinus filius Miecio*; *agentes inlustri viro Grimoaldo*; *per percepcione domno et geneture nostro Theuderico*; *in somnis Maximiano subdiacono*, ecc.,[1] con prevalenza del caso obliquo unico che si sostituisce al genitivo, quelli italiani dimostrano all'opposto una forte tendenza alla conservazione del genitivo classico, specie per quanto si riferisce ai nomi propri: *de tempore Cuniperti*; *manus Honorati filio quondam Vitaliani*; *Hermetruda filia Antonini*; *mea portione quamque et Rodoaldi germano meo*.[2] É opportuno rilevare che la prevalenza del caso obliquo unico nei documenti francesi non esclude affatto il genitivo classico, come quella del genitivo nei documenti italiani non esclude il caso unico. Se però si stabiliscono delle proporzioni più o meno

---

[1] Tardif, *Monuments historiques*, Paris, 1866; Lauer et Samaran, *Les diplômes originaux des Mérovingiens*, Paris, 1908; Pei, *The Language of the Eighth-Century Texts in Northern France*, New York, 1932, pp. 218-222.
[2] Bonelli, *Codice paleografico longobardo*, Milano, 1908.

esatte, si riscontra che mentre nei documenti francesi la forma obliqua unica prevale su quella del genitivo in ragione di quattro a uno, i documenti italiani offrono una leggera predominanza di forme classiche.

Si potrebbe obbiettare, specie da parte di coloro che credono poco al valore linguistico dei documenti di quell'epoca, che questo fenomeno è dovuto semplicemente al fatto che gli amanuensi italiani conservano la memoria della flessione latina in maggior grado che i francesi. Conviene pero opporre che questa ipotetica superiorità classica degli amanuensi italiani non si riscontra in alcum altro campo, né fonetico né morfologico; e pertanto, vien fatto piuttosto di pensare a un riflesso delle condizioni fonetiche delle due lingue in istato di formazione. Il francese, che tende già a far scomparire le vocali atone finali a eccezione dell'*a*, riunisce, foneticamente e morfologicamente, tutti i casi obliqui classici in una forma flessionale unica, che manterrà più tardi, per tutte le funzioni oblique, in contrasto col nominativo segnato da *-s* finale (*pro Deo amur, e por o fut presentede Maximiien*; *vindrent parent e lor amic, li Sanct Legier, li Evrui*; ecc.). L'italiano tende viceversa a conservare le vocali finali ed a sbarazzarsi delle consonanti. Non è possibile, per conseguenza, mantenere il contrasto tra *murus* e *murum* o *muro*; possibilissimo invece il mantenimento del genitivo *muri* contro la forma sincretica *muro* o *muru*. Ed è appunto questo genitivo in *-i* che rivela la sua tenace vitalità nei documenti italiani del secolo ottavo.

Passiamo ora al secolo nono. Nella *Carta abruzzese con tracce di volgare* pubblicata da Alfonso Gallo [3] troviamo ancora: ...*hofero ibit mea qui supra Pauli persona*...; *signu manus Dachenaldi filio Erfalani. Fluro filio Beneri. Calbulo filio Mauretani. Ursiniano filio Ursi.* Ci troviamo già all'epoca della comparsa dei primi documenti volgari francesi, nei quali il caso obliquo unico si sostituisce completamente al genitivo (*pro Deo amur*, dei Giuramenti di Strasburgo; *li Deo inimi, lo Deo menestier*, della Cantilena di Sant'Eulalia).

Veniamo ora al secolo decimo. Nelle formule testimoniali di Monte Cassino, [4] del tutto italiane, troviamo ancora *parte sancti Be-*

---

[3] *Bullettino dell'Istituto Storico Italiano e Archivio Muratoriano*, n. 45, 1929.

[4] Monteverdi, *Testi volgari italiani anteriori al Duecento*, Roma, 1935, pp. 15-18.

nedicti e *kella terra... sancte Marie è*. Escludiamoli pure ambedue dai nostri calcoli come facenti parte del formulario notarile; ma non potremo con eguale facilità sbarazzarci del *kelle terre... Pergoaldi foro* della formula testimoniale di Sessa del 963.

Parrebbe dunque assodato che agli albori della lingua italiana il genitivo classico resistesse ancora, per ragioni puramente fonetiche. È pur vero che a questo genitivo tendono a sostituirsi due tipi concorrenti: il caso unico in funzione di genitivo, come in Francia, e la formula sintattica colla preposizione *di*. Ma mentre questi due tipi trionfano sempre maggiormente per i sostantivi comuni (*duo congia de pulmentario faba et panico*, Archivio di Lucca, a. 765), il genitivo classico resta ancora in vigore per i nomi propri. Perché questa differenza di trattamento tra le due classi di sostantivi? Evidentemente perché nel nome comune il genitivo classico si confonderebbe col plurale (*muri-muri*), mentre nel nome di persona questo pericolo di confusione non esiste.

Seguiamo ora un po' nei primi secoli della lingua italiana, i destini dei tre tipi di genitivo (*filio Alberti*; *filio Alberto*; *filio de Alberto*), ai quali corrispondono, per necessità fonetiche, due soli tipi nell'antico francese (*li filz Rollant*; *li filz de Rollant*). È chiaro che la forma triplice debba dar luogo ad errori ed a confusioni, e di queste ci dànno abbondante esempio i documenti dei secoli XI e XII, prima che forma in *di* riesca ad assurgere ad un primato ancor oggi contrastato dalla forma irrigidita di molti cognomi italiani (*Giovanni Paoli, Giovanni de' Paoli, Giovanni di Paolo*):

Carta fabrianese (1186): [5] *...clesia santo Vectore et Rolando*; *...et de mo ad sante Marie de augusto...*; *...qui teni Martinu de Morico et Petri de Bonomo...*: caso unico che si sostituisce, senza preposizione, al genitivo; genitivo classico; caso unico con *de*; e, tanto per mostrare la confusione che genera la forma classica a fianco della nuova, il genitivo *Petri* in funzione di nominativo.

Carta picena (1193): [6] *... filius quondam Alberto Ofridi...*; *...in fundo la fonte Fracliti*; *...terra de Alberti Carvuni...*: caso unico senza preposizione in funzione di genitivo, seguito dal patronimico in *-i*; forma classica; forma classica coll'aggiunta della preposizione, seguita dal patronimico in *-i*.

---

[5] Monteverdi, pp. 49-51.
[6] Monteverdi, pp. 56-58.

Inventario fondano (sec. XII): [7] *... le cose de Antoni de Lupica...*; forma classica coll'aggiunta della preposizione.

Ritmo marchigiano di Sant'Alessio (sec. XII): [8] *... in templo sancti Boniphati loco forne portati...*; *... ket de genere era mperatore...*; latinismo forse il primo; caso unico in funzione di genitivo il secondo.

Carta di San Giminiano (1227): [9] *... anno tolto una peça di terra... che di sopera est Fidança, e di soto Atavante e filioli Guitocini... e est messere Rinieri dell'oche... e est filioli Geradini da Mottechi...*; *... testimonio Benisegna filiolo Titi, e Gunta fiolo Rafali, e Gunta filiolo Jovanni...* Già ci avviciniamo al Trecento, eppure in un documento completamente volgare troviamo ancora, se la parola *terra* è sottintesa, come sembra probabile, il caso unico in funzione di genitivo (*Atavante, messere Rinieri, filioli*), nonché il genitivo classico (*Guitocini, Geradini, Titi, Rafali*). Notisi però *dell'oche* per il sostantivo comune.

Il porco Sant'Antonio, il nodo Salamone, fi' Giovanni, la torre Babello, e le altre forme citate dal Pasquali per il Trecento sembrano dunque aver avuto una genealogia non soltanto abbastanza diretta, ma anche del tutto indigena, nonché, come dice il Pasquali, diffusa e popolare. Dove non possiamo trovarci d'accordo col Pasquali è nell'asserzione che il tipo "sembra limitato a nomi propri, il che mostra che esso già al principio della nostra letteratura era morto e non sopravviveva se non in formule irrigidite". È logico, viceversa, che il tipo che si riassume nella locuzione *in casa i Frescobaldi* si riscontri, come espressione popolare e vivente, appunto nei nomi propri, gli unici che siano stati in grado di conservare più a lungo, senza tema di confusione col plurale, la forma del genitivo latino, e, di conseguenza, anche il primo surrogato di quella forma, cioè il caso unico senza preposizione.

Non sarà il caso di andare a cercare l'origine della locuzione nei francesismi trecenteschi: la formula *in casa i Frescobaldi* sembra piuttosto la continuazione logica ed italianissima delle forme citate

---

[7] Monteverdi, pp. 62-64.
[8] Monteverdi, p. 75.
[9] Monaci, *Crestomazia italiana dei primi secoli*, Città di Castello, 1912, p. 31.

sopra. Che poi si sia estesa per analogia fino al boccaccesco *a casa le buone femmine* non dovrebbe arrecarci soverchia sorpresa.

Vi è piuttosto un'altra questione interessante da risolvere. C'è da fidarsi dell'articolo *i* nell'espressione suddetta? Potrebbe darsi il caso che *in casa (i) Frescobaldi* rappresentasse piuttosto il genitivo singolare, anziché la forma unica plurale usata in funzione di genitivo? L'evoluzione che abbiamo tracciata consentirebbe entrambe le ipotesi.

Lingua Nostra, I (August, 1939)

VI

FRENCH -*IER* FROM LATIN -*ARIU*

The arising of the French suffix -*ier*, -*ière* out of an original Latin -*ariu*, -*aria* is one of the most controversial points in Romance linguistics.[1] While theories are as numerous and varied as the scholars who advance them, it is possible to classify them in five general groups:

1. -*ariu*, with transposition of the *i* in hiatus that becomes *i̯* in Vulgar Latin, turns into *-*airu*; the diphthong *ai* becomes *e*, and this *e*, endowed with open quality, joins the general development of Classical Latin free short stressed *e* and diphthongizes into *ie* (-*ariu* > *-*airu* > *-*ęru* > *ier*). This theory, advanced by Schuchardt,[2] is elaborated upon by Meyer-Lübke,[3] who attempts to establish a chronological differentiation in development between -*ariu* > -*ier* and -*aria* > -*aire* (Latin *area* > French *aire*, etc.), with -*ière* arising from analogy of -*ier*.

Apart from the objection that *variu* gives OF *vair*, not *vier, the crucial phonological difficulty with this theory is that Old French regularly preserves the diphthong *ai*, and does not reduce it, even in pronunciation, to the monophthong *ę* until at least the end of the eleventh century;[4] -*ier*, on the other hand, appears as early as the *Eulalie*. Additional difficulty is presented by the fact that in Spa-

---

[1] For a complete discussion and evaluation of the hypotheses that have been advanced, cf. E. R. Zimmermann, *Die Geschichte des lateinischen Suffixes -arius in den romanischen Sprachen*, Darmstadt, 1895; and E. Staaf, *Le suffixe -arius dans les langues romanes*, Upsal, 1896.

[2] *Vokalismus des Vulgärlateins*, II, 454, 521, 528.

[3] *Grammaire des langues romanes*, § 235, § 522.

[4] Schwan-Behrens, *Grammaire de l'ancien français*, I, § 56, I; § 223.

nish, where the transposition of i̯ and the merging of *ai* into *e* is definitely established, the resulting monophthong is from the very outset treated as closed *e*, not as open *e*; the tenth-century Glosses of San Millán offer *terzero* < *tertiariu* side by side with such diphthongized forms as *tienet, buena mientre, liebat, sieculos* (Italian forms in *-iere, ieri, -iero*, which were at one time thought to have had a native development along the same lines as French *-ier* are now generally admitted to be of imported French or Provençal origin; [5] this belief appears likely not only because of the nature of the words in question, but also by reason of the fact that such forms do not appear before the twelfth century [6]). Acceptance of the Schuchardt-Meyer-Lübke theory therefore involves: 1. a phonological change of *ai* > *e*, occurring exclusively in the group *-airu*, at a period when this change is otherwise unattested in French; 2. a treatment of this *e* as open *e*, with consequent diphthongization into *ie*, contrary to what occurs in other sections of Romance territory, notably Spain and Portugal, where the *e* resulting from *ai* is closed. French, and perhaps Provençal, would therefore have a development which is not only unique in all Romania, but at variance with their own normal phonological evolution.

2. *-ariu*, which would normally give *-er* or *-eir*, is influenced by the numerous forms in which it is preceded by i̯ or a palatal; the development of *-ariu* into *-ier* is thus partly phonological, partly analogical. This hypothesis, first advanced by Gaston Paris, [7] is, with certain modifications, adopted by Cohn, [8] Zimmermann, [9] and accepted by Darmesteter, Brunot, Nyrop and others.

The principal objections to it are: 1. that *-iariu*, had it developed to *-iairu*, *-ieiru*, should ultimately have been reduced to *-ir*,

---

[5] D'Ovidio & Meyer-Lübke, *Grammatica storica della lingua e dei dialetti italiani*, p. 86; Grandgent, *From Latin to Italian*, § 24, 2; Staaf, pp. 132-151.

[6] The form *rasteliero* < *rastellariu*, appearing in a document of Ravenna of the year 752, is reported by Fantuzzi, *Monumenti ravennati*, Venezia, 1801-1804, IV, 155, and cited by Gloria, *Del volgare illustre*, Venezia, 1880, p. 115. Considerable doubt attaches, however, to the authenticity and proper dating of Fantuzzi's collection.

[7] *Romania*, IX, 330.

[8] *Die Suffixwandelung im Vulgärlatein und im vorlitterarischen Französisch*, p. 274 ff.

[9] *Op. cit.*

not to -*ier*; 2. that it fails to account for Provençal and southwestern French -*eir*, -*er* forms.

3. The theory of a "psychological" replacement of -*ariu* in the Vulgar Latin period by -*ęriu* is advanced in considerable detail by Gröber.[10] Original Latin words in -*ĕriu*, joined by those in -*ēriu*, according to this theory extended their sway over the -*ariu* forms, giving rise to French -*ier* and Italian -*iere*, -*ieri*, *iero*. This theory, with modifications, is restated by Marchot,[11] Skok,[12] and, for Provençal, by Crescini;[13] the latter author, commenting upon the double and triple forms of Provençal (*empeir, empier* < *imperiu*; *feira, fieira, fiera* < *feria*) suggests a double development: -*ariu* > -*ęriu* > -*eir* > on the one hand -*ieir*, -*ir* and on the other -*er*.

Objections to this suffix-substitution theory are: 1. words with an -*ĕriu* suffix, even with the reenforcement of -*ēriu*, are far less numerous and popular in Latin than -*ariu* words; attraction should logically have worked in the opposite direction; 2. French forms such as *archer, berger*, etc. indicate development of the palatal as before *a*, not as before *e*; 3. there is little ground for admitting that -*ĕriu* was joined by -*ēriu* before the dawn of the Romance period; words with the latter suffix display normal *ē* tendencies in the Merovingian and early Carolingian documents[14] instead of the *ĕ* tend-

---

[10] "Vulgärlateinische Substrate romanischer Wörter", *Archiv für lateinische Lexicographie*, I, 204 ff.

[11] *Solution de quelques difficultés de la phonétique française*; also ZRP, XVII, 288; XIX, 61.

[12] *ZPR*, LIV, 187-191. Skok presents the following attractive hypothesis: the Greek suffix -ηριον, with original open pronunciation of Greek η, gives rise, in loan-words borrowed by Latin, particularly those of a religious nature (*psaltērium, monastērium, plastērium, potērium, baptistērium*, etc.) to a Vulgar Latin -*ęriu*, which Christianity, at a period of intense religious activity, extends even to non-Romance languages (Serbo-Croatian *molstir*). The psychological force of this religious -*ęriu* is sufficient to bring about a widespread replacement of -*ariu*. Unfortunately, the handling of Greek η in Latin is by no means consistent (cf. Grandgent, *Introduction to Vulgar Latin*, § 182); closed *e* and even *i* developments appear in Vulgar Latin and Romance somewhat more frequently than open *e* ones; cf. also *infra* note 14.

[13] *Manuale per l'avviamento agli studi provenzali*, pp. 39-40.

[14] Cf. Pei, *The Language of the Eighth-Century Texts in Northern France*. pp. 20-25, 364; the word *monastērium* displays the customary Vulgar Latin tendency to change *ē* to *i* (*monestirio, monasthyrio*, etc.), while *ĕ* regularly remains unchanged; yet this word subsequently develops into the

ency to remain unchanged; 4. in French, the normal phonological outcome of *-ĕriu* should be **-ieir*, **-ir*; that of *ēriu* should be **-eir*; in neither case *-ier*; 5. if, in accordance with Gröber's views, Italian *-iere, -iero* is taken to be a native development of *-ĕriu*, the question arises why the Italian outcome is not **-ieio*, in accordance with normal Italian development, which presents *-aio* < *-ariu* and *-uoio* < *-oriu*.

4. Other substitution theories are advanced by Ascoli,[15] who supposes a Vulgar Latin form **-aeru*, and by Horning,[16] who supposes a replacement of *-arius* by *-aris*. The first replacement form appears extremely hypothetical, while the second is open to the same objection as that of the replacement of *-ariu* by *-ęriu*; the *-arius* suffix is far stronger and more popular than the *-aris*.

5. The supposition of a Germanic influence in the French development is advanced by A. Thomas.[17] Germanic proper names in *-aris*, assimilated in Vulgar Latin to the *-arius* type, but subject to an umlaut tendency which turns the *a* into *e*, are said by Thomas to have influenced the entire course of development of *-ariu*, turning it into *-eru*, with open *e*, then into *-ier*. This view is accepted by Anglade.[18]

To this theory it may be objected that if the Germanic proper names in question joined the *-ariu* class, as they undoubtedly did, they would be more likely to follow the destinies of that class than to impose their own original Germanic phonological laws upon them; this supposition appears substantiated by the accent-shift whereby the original Germanic stress on the initial syllable is lost, to be replaced by a stress which follows Latin-Romance laws of accentuation (*Hlódhari* > *Ludhér*; *Théuderich* > *Thierrý*; *Húgun* > *Hugóne* > *Huón*, etc.). Between the fifth-century conquest of France by the Germanic invaders and the arising of the umlaut tendency in question, which most Germanic linguists seem disposed

---

monstier of early Old French, indicating a shift to the *-ier* group, from whatever source this may have come, at the outset of the Old French period.

[15] *Archivio glottologico italiano*, I, 484; IX, 381; X, 104.

[16] *ZRP*, XII, 580.

[17] "L'Evolution phonétique du suffixe -arius en Gaule", *Bausteine zur romanischen Philologie, Festgabe für A. Mussafia*, pp. 641-661; also *Romania*, XXXI, 481.

[18] *Grammaire de l'ancien français*, pp. 48-49.

to place toward the beginning of the eighth century, [19] the proper names which had joined the -*arius* class may be supposed to have achieved a certain stability within that class which removed them from the phonological tendencies of the mother-tongue. The point made by Thomas (page 659) that the few forms in Vulgar Latin documents which appear in this connection generally have -*ero*, not -*erio*, [20] undoubtedly militates against the Gröber-Marchot theory of a substitution of -*ĕriu* for -*ariu*, but is not in itself a proof of Germanic umlaut influence, since the form -*ero* can be explained in other and perhaps more satisfactory ways, as will be seen below.

The above enumeration by no means exhausts the theories and combinations of theories that have been advanced in connection with French -*ier*, but presents the main currents of thought. It is also to be noted that several authorities decline to take a stand in the matter, and limit themselves to describing the development as abnormal. [21]

* * *

A new possibility that presents itself is that the suffix -*ariu*, in certain sections of France and in certain classes of words, may have been reduced to -*aru*, with loss of the $i̯$ instead of transposition; that this -*aru*, in accordance with normal French phonological processes, may have developed into -*er*, with open *e*; and that this open *e*, at a time when diphthongization of stressed vowels was beginning, may have been partially confused with original free short stressed Latin *e*, and have diphthongized into *ie*, again in accordance with normal French phonological processes. The attraction by the stronger -*aru* type of the less numerous and popular -*ĕriu*, -*ēriu* classes, with or without previous reduction to *-*ĕru*, *-*ēru*, may then be assumed.

The first part of this theory is by no means new. Marchot claims passage of -*ariu* to -*aru*, but thinks that subsequently -*aru* is repla-

---

[19] J. Schatz, *Althochdeutsche Grammatik*, p. 39; W. Waltemath, *Die fränkischen Elemente in der französischen Sprache*, pp. 47-48.

[20] *Berhero*, not *Berherio*, in a document of 766; *sorcerus* and *paner* in the Glosses of Reichenau; 35 proper names in -*erus*, -*era* in the Polyptique d'Irminon, as against 600 forms in -*arius*, -*aria*, and only one form in -*erius*.

[21] Bourciez, *Eléments de linguistique romane*, § 264 b; Zauner, *Romanische Sprachwissenschaft*, I, § 237; Schwan-Behrens, *Grammaire de l'ancien français*, § 56, 2; etc.

ced by *-eru*. Zimmermann also supposes *-ariu* > *-aru*, but then accounts for *-ier* by the analogy of forms in which *i̯* or a palatal precedes the *a*. Since *-ariu* turns to *-aru* in a large section of the Romance field (*-ariu* > *-aio* in Tuscany, but > *-aro* in most dialects of northern and southern Italy; [22] Roumanian forms in *-ar* also appear best explained as coming from *-aru*), there seems to be no good reason for disputing the possibility of *-ariu* > *-aru* on French soil as well. The fall of vowels in hiatus, which some linguists attempt to restrict to certain specific combinations, appears to be fairly general whenever the change from pure *i* or *u* to semivowels leads to combinations difficult to pronounce. [23] A list of Vulgar Latin forms in which *-aru* replaces *-ariu* is offered by Schuchardt [24] and repeated by Staaf, [25] who, however, refuses to admit that *-aru* may, in the course of time, have replaced *-ariu* everywhere (it may be remarked that it is not at all necessary to admit universal replacement; a partial tendency, in certain localities, suffices). The appearance of *-er* instead of *-ier* in several Old French manuscripts [26] is suggested by Cohn as partial proof of *-aru* for *-ariu* on northern French soil.

It may be well at this point to review the general evidence of the documents of the pre-French period in connection with the suffix

---

[22] Meyer-Lübke, *Grammaire*, § 521.

[23] Cf. Grandgent, *Introduction to Vulgar Latin*, § 222-227; he offers not only *arietem* > *aretem*, *parietes* > *paretes*, *quietus* > *quetus*, *battuo* > *batto* and *coquo* > *coco*, but also *torqueo* > **torquo* > **torco*; Bourciez, *Eléments*, § 84, describes the tendency to drop *i̯* in *-eo* and *-io* verbs and offers **sento* and **dormo*; his suggestion that these forms may have been created by analogy of the other forms of the verb appears invalidated by the numerous other verbs in which this analogy does not take place, by his statement (§ 290 b) to the effect that in Provençal verbs in *-io* generally lose the *i̯*, and by his examples of double forms such as *au*, *auch*, *fau*, *fatz*, *cre*, *crei*. These double forms are of special interest because they show the tendency to drop *i̯* on Gallic soil, side by side, with the tendency to retain it. Additional Vulgar Latin forms in which *i* and *u* in hiatus are lost are reported by Muller & Taylor, *Chrestomathy of Vulgar Latin*, p. 37; particularly interesting because they show the fall of *i̯* before *u* in French territory are *sacerdotum* for *sacerdotium* (Gregory of Tours) and *homicidum* for *homicidium* (Frodebertus and Importunus).

[24] *Vokalismus*, II, 451.

[25] *Op. cit.*, pp. 11-12.

[26] *Chevaler—Roland*; *primer—Passion de Sainte Catherine*; *encensers—Ami et Amile*; etc.; cf. also Zimmermann, p. 44.

-ariu. The conservation of this suffix is quite general. The forms in *-aru* cited by Schuchardt are nevertheless compelling (*cancellarus, carbonaru, casarus, cornicularus, tabellarus, Febraras, Ianuaras,* etc.). As against these fairly numerous forms, we have a doubtful sixth-century *glanderia* (< *glandarius* + *-ia?*) reported by Grandgent. [27] Seventh and eighth-century texts indicate an overwhelming survival of *-ariu*, in Germanic proper names as well as in common nouns (*Theodaharius, Vualacharium, Chrodchario, Rotgarius, Chlodocharius* are a few specimens taken at random from Tardif's eighth-century *Monuments historiques*. The only form that affords evidence in favor of the transposition theory is Pirson's *concambitairas* for *concambitarias*; [28] this isolated occurrence may perhaps be ascribed to a slip of the pen. The interchange of *Amalgero* and *Amalgario* (year 679), reported by Vielliard, [29] and a similar case in Tardif (no. 68, year 770 —*Hartgario*; no. 78, year 777— *Hartgero*) are admittedly doubtful because of the possibility of two different Germanic suffixes. *Berhero* for *Berhario* (year 766), and the Irminon Polyptique's 35 forms in *-ero, -era*, reported by Thomas, [30] are not at all in conflict with the theory of a passage from *-ariu* to *-aru* and then to *-eru, -er*, but rather support it (let us not forget, however, the 600 forms in *-arius, -aria*, also appearing in the Polyptique, indicating the strong vitality of the old suffix, which yields only occasionally to pronunciation difficulties, or the one form in *-erius*, which may display change of *a* to *e* in the original suffix; and let us also recall the probability that the two suffixes *-arius* and *-acus* were in the forefront of the change from *a* to *e*). [31]

As we advance to the dawn of the Romance period, we find *sorcerus* (for **sortiarius*) and *paner* in the Glosses of Reichenau. The Glosses, however, also contain at least 40 forms in *-arius* (*uolumptarius, berbicarius, carpentarii, panario, ostiarii, cellarius, lectarium, chaldaria, manaria, plumarii, incensarium, butillarius,*

---

[27] *Introduction to Vulgar Latin*, § 39.

[28] *Romanische Forschungen*, XXVI, 919.

[29] *La Langue des diplômes royaux et chartes privées de l'époque mérovingienne*, pp. 3, 61.

[30] Cf. also Cipriani, *Etude sur quelques noms propres d'origine germanique*, Angers, 1901.

[31] Cf. Pei, *op. cit.*, pp. 15-16, and Morel, *Etude sur la langue des chartes de Cluny, Xe siècle*, Ecole des Chartes, 1914, p. 77.

focarias, arcarius, etc.), which are generally disregarded by linguists who seek in documentary evidence only those phenomena which indicate change. As against these forms, *ministerium, ministerio, desiderium,* etc., seem to indicate no confusion between the *-ariu* and the *-eriu* suffixes. So far as *sorcerus* and *paner* are concerned, there appears to be no difficulty in deriving them from **sortiaru* and **panaru.*

The Rhaeto-Romance (?) Glosses of Cassel show *sestar, caldaru* and *paioari,* all of which indicate origin from *-aru* forms, side by side with the conservative *siluuarias* and with what appears to be a transposed development in *manneiras.*

Lastly, the *Ludher* (< *Hlodhari*) of the Oaths of Strasbourg indicates fair *-aru* possibilities.

* * *

If *-ariu* passed to *-aru,* wholly or partly, the question then arises whether the *a* of *-aru* could have turned into *e* with open quality, and whether the ρ thus formed could have diphthongized to *ie.*

The controversy regarding the original sound of Old French *e* < Latin *a* need not be gone into in detail at this point.[32] Considering the starting-point of the sound-shift, Böhmer's contention that the *e* arising from *a* was intermediate between *a* and ρ seems more acceptable than Gaston Paris' hypothesis that it was extremely closed.[33] If the *e* resulting from Latin free *a* was originally, in the formative period of the language, an open one, as is the opinion of Böhmer, Schwan-Behrens, Bourciez and others, then the possibility, in that period of flux and uncertainty, of occasional

---

[32] Cf. Meyer-Lübke, *Grammaire,* § 225, for the more important details; a distinction among the *e*'s arising in Old French from Latin *a,* from Latin *ĕ* and from Latin *ē* is claimed by Gaston Paris, *Saint Alexis,* p. 49 ff., by Böhmer, *Romanische Studien,* 1, 5, 599 ff., and by others; there is, however, absolutely no agreement as to the nature of the sounds, particularly that of *e* < *a.* As illustrations of the opinions of authorities, we may cite Bourciez, *Eléments,* § 263 a, who says that the primitive sound of *e* < *a* was undoubtedly a long, open ρ; and Schwan-Behrens, § 35, § 52, § 211, who claim *a* > long ρ, this, with the fall of final vowels, > closed *ē.*

[33] Cf. Lücking, *Die ältesten französischen Mundarten,* Berlin, 1877, pp. 91-106, for a full description of the evidence, and for conclusions with which we can hardly agree.

confusion with ę from Latin ĕ appears likely, and this contention seems borne out by the earliest monuments of French.

An independent survey of assonances and forms in the oldest French literary works establishes the following points: [34]

EULALIE

-ariu and *-ĕriu* have fallen together and developed into *-ier;* the diphthong appears in assonance with *ie* < *ĕ* and with *ie* < palatal + *a:* 5-6: *conselliers:ciel;* 9-10: *pleier:menestier;* 25-26: *ciel:preier.* The fact that no assonance of this sound with *e* < *a* appears may be accidental, in a 29-line poem in which only one *e* < *a* assonance occurs (17-18: *virginitet:honestet*).

FRAGMENT DE VALENCIENNES

Scanty evidence is to be derived from this document because of its fragmentary nature and lack of assonances. No *-ariu* or *-eriu* forms appear. 11: *cheve* and 29: *cherte* seem to indicate lack of diphthongization into *ie* of palatal + *a.* Of more definite interest are the forms 15: *eedre* (but 12, 17: *edre*) and 28: *peer.* If the former is interpreted as indicating the initial stage of diphthongization of *ę* < free *ĕ,* the same supposition would seem reasonable for the latter (the form *piers* appears in the *Léger;* cf. *infra*). But this would be a case of the diphthong *ie* arising from original Latin *a* not preceded by a palatal.

PASSION DU CHRIST

This poem is even more unsatisfactory, from the point of view of evidence, because of its Provençal admixture. A few forms in *-ariu,* rendered as *-er,* appear (38: *olivers;* 85: *deners;* 377: *primers;* 419: *primera*), while one is rendered as *-eir* (190: *useire*). The only

---

[34] References to the *Eulalie, Fragment, Passion* and *Léger* are to lines in Koschwitz's *Les Plus Anciens Monuments de la langue française,* Leipzig, 1913; references to the *Alexis* are to *laisses* in Förster & Koschwitz's *Altfranzösisches Übungsbuch,* Leipzig, 1915; references to the *Roland* are to *laisses* in T. A. Jenkins' *Chanson de Roland,* Heath, 1924.

form in assonance is *primers:pecchiad*, of which the French original is likely to have been *primiers:pechiet*, with equivalence of *ie* < *-ariu* and *ie* < palatal + *a*.

A few additional assonances appear which may indicate confusion of sounds; but not very much reliance can be placed in them in view of the linguistic mixture:

7-8: *deus:carnals*; if this represents *deus:charnels*, we have equivalence of *e* < *ĕ* and *e* < *a* (but cf. *infra* for *deu*).

43-44: *mantenls:pez*; if this represents *mantels:pez* or *piez*, we have equivalence of *e* < checked *ĕ* and *e* or *ie* < free *ĕ*.

105-106: *pietad:parler*; if this represents *pitiet:parler*, we have equivalence of *ie* < palatal + *a* and *e* < *a* (but cf. *infra* for *pitiet, pitet*).

409-410: *anunciaz:oblidez*; if this represents *annunciez:oblidez*, we have equivalence of *ie* < palatal + *a* and *e* < *a*.

LÉGER

Here we find again the equivalence of *ie* < *ĕ*, palatal + *a*, *-ariu* and *-eriu* that appears in the *Eulalie*: 5-6: *biens:lethgier*; 19-20: *peitieus:lothiers*; 65-66: *clergier: monstier*; 97-98: *voluntiers:monstier*; 103-104: *mistier:castier*.

To this is added very frequent diphthongization of *e* < *a* without preceding palatal. This *ie* < *a* appears in assonance with *e* < *a*, and even with *a* (retained by learned or Provençal influence?), but not with *ie* from other sources: 33-34: *caritet:veritiet*; 41-42: *laudiez: amet*; 59-60: *piers:gred*; 101-102: *miel:el*; 123-124: *miel:anatemaz*; 135-136: *miel:observer*; 141-142: *ciutat-miel*; 159-160: *vituperet: miels*; 171-172: *carnels:spiritiel*; 181-182: *restaurat:laudier*; 215-216: *spiritiel:perdonat*.

On the other hand, definite equivalence appears between *e* and *ie* < *ĕ*, *-ariu*, *-eriu* and palatal + *a*: 81-82: *mistier:ben*; 121-122: *bien:evesquet*; 157-158: *talier:queu*; 223-224: *1. (lethgier* or *lothier):pez*; 229-230: *queu:pez*.

ie < palatal + checked *ĕ* is in assonance with *e* < checked *ĕ*: 179-180: *flaiel:seruu*; 193-194: *flaiel:laudebert*.

In the case of one word, *deu*, we find a strange equivalence to practically all possible values of *e* and *ie*:

ie < palatal + *a*: 147-148: *preier:deu*.

e < *a*: 201-202: *claritet:deu*.

e, ie, < *ĕ:* 207-208: *deus:ciel;* 237-238: *dominedeus:cel.*

The diphthongization into *ie* of *e* < *a* without preceding palatal is a striking characteristic of the *Léger:* 34: *veritiet;* 36: *humilitiet;* 172: *spiritiels;* 215: *spiritiel;* 65, 144, 207, etc.: *tiel* (as against 138: *tal;* 73: *tel,* etc.); 59: *piers;* 161, 169: *parlier;* 167, 184: *porlier;* 129, 160, etc.: *miels* (as against 114: *mala*); 101, 123, 135, 144, etc.: *miel;* 162, 168: *laudier;* 41: *laudiez.*

Non-diphthongization of *e* < free *ĕ* or palatal + *a* is also frequent, but not to the same degree: 82: *ben;* 122: *evesquet;* 158, 229: *queu;* 148, 202: *deu;* 207, 237: *deus;* 238: *cel;* 224, 230: *pez;* etc.

The diphthongization of *e* < *a* without preceding palatal is far from being without parallel in later documents, as will be seen below. Its extreme frequency in the *Léger,* however, has elicited comment from various sources. Diez [35] calls attention to the phenomenon, but makes no attempt to explain it; he is somewhat in favor of the theory that the poem may have originated in Poitou; Champollion-Figeac [36] had already suggested Limousin or Poitou, while Du Méril [37] had suggested Normandy. Suchier [38] claims Walloon origin, but is controverted by Gaston Paris, [39] who rejects all preceding ideas, including that of Poitevin and that of a mixture of French and Provençal, and claims Autun in Burgundy as the most probable home of the *Léger* original; in connection with the diphthongization into *ie* of *e* < *a,* Paris points out that *ie* appears also for *ei* (23-24: *savier:fied;* 53-54: *fiet:rei*), and suggests that the apparent *ie* < *a* is nothing but an error on the part of a Bourguignon scribe who is attempting to render the *ei*-sound of his own dialect (but *ie* appears also for original long *i:* 139-140: *civ:asalier*). Lücking [40] also attempts to explain the forms in *ie* < *a* on the theory of scribal error, but prefers the view that the scribe is a Provençal attempting to render French sounds.

---

[35] *Zwei altromanische Gedichte,* Bonn, 1852.
[36] *Documents historiques inédits,* Paris, 1841-1848, IV, 446.
[37] *Essai philosophique sur la formation de la langue française,* Paris 1852, p. 414.
[38] *ZRP,* II, 255.
[39] *Romania,* I, 273 ff.; VII, 629.
[40] *Op. cit.,* p. 73.

It may be added, in connection with the problem of diphthongization in the *Léger,* that *ie* appears very frequently in the demonstrative adjective-pronouns (20, 49, 56, etc.: *ciel;* 13, 32, etc.: *ciels;* 207: *ciest;* etc.; forms with the normal *e* are slightly more numerous). The identical phenomenon (*ciest, cieste*) appears in a Bourguignon (Côte-d'Or) document of 1278, offerend by Schwan-Behrens,[41] who advance no explanation whatsoever for it. And while it is perhaps unsafe to advance the evidence of modern dialects in connection with the developments of the Old French period, it may be remarked that diphthongized forms of the demonstrative appear today in various sections.[42] The point is not relevant in connection with *e* or *ie* < *a,* but does indicate that it is perhaps unwise to refer to scribal errors all forms in the older documents which do not fit in with rigid so-called "phonological laws".

ALEXIS

Equivalence of *e* or *ie* < free *ĕ*, *-ariu, -eriu,* palatal + *a* appears: 11: *anuitet:colcer:ciel:corocier:muiler;* 25: *anterciet:ciel:provenders:almosners:liez;* 36: *muster:antercier:set:ciel:esluiner;* etc.

In the case of two words, *eret* (or *ieret*) and *deu, e, ie* < free *ĕ* is in assonance with *e* < *a:* 4: *pedre:ieret:emperere:honurede:cuntretha;* 18: *ciptet:parler:deu:salvetet:deu;* 34: *afermet:citied:parler:alter:deu;* 48: *medra:espusede:aviserent:demanderent:eret;* 76: *aneret:esculterent:medre:eret:truvede;* 109: *volentet:oneuret:citet:deu:aluez.*

Gaston Paris points out in his study of the *Alexis* that *deu* and *eret,* despite their original *ĕ,* join the *e* < *a.* We have seen in the *Léger,* however, that *deu* is in assonance on the one hand with *e* < *a* (*claritet*), on the other with *ie* < palatal + *a* (*preier*), and with *e, ie* < free *ĕ* (*ciel, cel*).

In one *laisse,* 65, we have the equivalence of *e* < *a* with *e* < checked *ĕ: set* (< *sapit*)*:alet:aprester:menestrels:set.*

---

[41] *Op. cit.,* III, 54-56.
[42] *Cieutx*—Mathanvilliers, Brezolles, Perche—Herzog, *Neufranzösische Dialekttexte,* Leipzig, 1914, pp. 60-61; *thieu, thielle, thiés*—Niort, Poitou—Herzog, p. 53; *tyet, kyet* and similar forms—Vendée, Deux-Sèvres, Vienne, Charente, Charente Inférieure, Gironde—*Atlas linguistique,* p. 44.

Diphthongization of $e < a$ without preceding palatal appears occasionally in the *Alexis:* 34: *citied;* 21: *citiet;* Introduction: *trinitiet;* Appendix: *asemblier. Citiet,* in 21, in assonance with *medra, espusethe, alet, demenet,* appears in contrast with *citet,* in 118, which is in assonance with *parez, poser, poestet* and *atarger. Atarger* itself is a form in which *ie* < palatal + *a* should have developed, and which should not be in assonance with $e < a$, if the distinction between the two sounds were a clear-cut one at this period.

Fairly frequently, diphthongization fails to occur in $e <$ free $\breve{e}$, *-ariu, -eriu,* palatal + *a:* Introduction: *amistet;* 11: *colcer; muiler;* 25: *provenders, almosners* 36; *set* (< *sedet*); 76: *eret* (as against 4: *ieret*); 52: *volenters* (as against 68 *volentiers*).

Lücking's conclusion [43] is that, just as the scribe of the *Léger* is a Provençal who does not know how to render French sounds, so also the scribe of the Lambspringe *Alexis* is an Anglo-Saxon whose ignorance of French is responsible for his errors. If this view is correct, it is indeed unfortunate that so many of the few early monuments of the French tanguage should have come down to us in the versions of non-Frenchmen who were unacquainted with the language in which they were writing.

ROLAND

The customary equivalence of *ie* < free $\breve{e}$, *-ariu, -eriu,* palatal + *a* appears: III: *chevaliers:aidier:fier:amistiez:chiens:bien,* etc.; VIII: *liez:chevalier:vergier:fiers:enseignier,* etc.; XXXVI: *tient:nies:otreier: liiez:destrier:somier,* etc.; CXXXI: *chastiier:Oliviers:mestier:mielz: venguier:liet:somiers:pitiet:mostiers,* etc.

Deu, despite its original $\breve{e}$, is in assonance with $e < a$. A form *chevaler* (instead of *chevalier*) also appears in $e < a$ assonance: IX: *parlet:deu:adorer:doner:deu:penser,* etc.; XXVII: *ostel:recovrer:fermez:damnedeu:chevaler:per,* etc.; CCIII: *entrez:plorer:aler:chevaler: champels:ber,* etc.

$e < a$ appears in *ie* assonance in CCXLIII: *fieres:brisiedes:chrestiene:jostede:otreiede,* etc.

---

[43] *Op. cit.,* pp. 73-75.

In XL we find both *e* and *ie* < palatal + *a* in *e* < *a* assonance: *parler:passet:mendistet:osteier:tels:ber:barnet*, etc., while the very next *laisse*, XLI, shows us *osteier* and *mendistiet* in their more normal *ie* < *ĕ*, *-ariu*, *-eriu*, palatal + *a* assonance: *merveillier:vielz: mielz:travailliet:mendistiet:osteier:nies:ciel:chevaliers*, etc.

Bocler and *bacheler* (< **bucculare*, **baccalare*, or < **bucculariu*, **baccalariu* ?) both appear. The second is not in assonance, while the first is in *e* < *a* assonance: CXLVI: *ber:boclers:desmembrer:oblider:per:jostez*, etc. Both these words appear in later works with the *-ier* ending.

Other cases of hesitation between *e* and *ie* forms appear, in addition to the *chevaler-chevalier* and *mendistet-mendistiet* mentioned above. *Pitet* (not in assonance; LXVI) is in contrast with *pitiet* (in *ie* assonance; CXXXI, CLXII). Four forms with apparent *ie* < *a* without preceding palatal appear: *seiet* (< *setatu*; not in assonance; CCXXXI); *ormier* (< *aure mare* (?); [44] in regular *ie* assonance; VIII, CIII, CXVII, CLXXXIV); *iriez, iriet* (< *iratu*; in regular *ie* assonance; CXVII, CLX, CLXXVI); *destorbier* (for *destorber*; in regular *ie* assonance; CIII).

The general conclusions to which we are led by the evidence at our disposal are the following:

The *e* or *ie* arising out of *ĕ*, *-ariu*, *-eriu* and palatal + *a* are equal. They do not, for the most part, coincide with *e* or *ie* < *a* without preceding palatal. There are, however, enough instances of coincidence to indicate a certain amount of confusion in pronunciation.

The entire matter of diphthongization of *e* into *ie*, from whatever source the *e* may come (free *ĕ*, *-ariu*, *-eriu*, *a* with or without preceding palatal) appears to be in a state of flux up to the eleventh century, with ultimate standardization fairly, but not completely, established by the time of the *Roland*.

Forms in which *e* < *ĕ*, *-ariu*, *-eriu*, palatal + *a* does not diphthongize are numerous; equally numerous are forms in which *ie* develops from *a* without preceding palatal. Both phenomena appear

---

[44] But cf. for this form J. D. M. Ford, *Speculum*, II (1927), 97, who claims derivation from *aurum merum*, and also disputes the reading *chevaler* of *laisses* XXVII and CCIII, preferring *bacheler*.

too often and in too many works to be explained away by the theory of scribal error. It would appear that for the forms in question we must either admit confusion and hesitation in pronunciation, or start from two different original bases for each word, one with, the other without i̯; which, far from contradicting the first hypothesis, simply pushes it back into the pre-French period. Confusion and hesitation in pronunciation, particularly in a period of linguistic instability, are not surprising phenomena. We need only refer to the evidence of the *Roland*, at the end of the period in question, for a most clear-cut example of such confusion: the orthographic diphthong *ai* appears sometimes in *a* assonances, indicating the diphthongal value of *á* + i̯ (*laisses* XX, LVIII, LX, LXVII, LXXXVI, CLXXI); at other times in *e* < checked *ĕ* assonances, indicating the monophthongal value of *e̬* (IV, XLVI, LIII, LXXV, CVIII, CXXVII, CLVI, CLXVI, CLXVII, CLXXXI, CCVIII).

The earliest monuments of French are not the only ones in which *ie* < *a* without preceding palatal appears. *Pier* < *pare* is to be found elsewhere than in the *Léger*; [45] so also *tiel*. [46] *Pieu* < *palu*, which survives to the present day, is reported by Gamillscheg [47] as early as the twelfth century (are we quite certain that the explanation offered by Schwan-Behrens, § 211, is the correct one, and that diphthongization of *e* set in only after the change of *l* to *u* in such forms as *pieu, tieus, ostieus*, when we consider the *miel, tiel* and *spiritiel* of the *Léger* ?). The dialectal versions of the Sermons of Maurice de Sully present frequent occurrences of *parlier, beautié, chantié, abbié, appeliez, passiez, estié, quiel*, etc., as against *volunters, encensers, noer, premere*. [48]

The evidence seems to point to a tendency toward diphthongization of *e* < *a* without preceding palatal (whatever its pronunciation may have been). That this phenomenon may in origin have been dialectal, and have spread irregularly, attaching itself more definitely to certain forms and suffixes and dropping out of others as the

---

[45] Ben. D. de Norm., II, 17402; Foulques Fitz Warin, *Nouv. fr. du XIV⁰ s.*, p. 48.
[46] Rendus de Moil. *Clarité*, IX, 5; *Chron. de S. Den.*, ms. Ste-Gen., f. 55ᵈ vº; Oresme; and cf. Godefroy, *Dictionnaire, s. v.*
[47] *Etymologisches Wörterbuch der französischen Sprache, s. v.*
[48] Cf. P. Meyer, *Romania*, v, 466 ff.

language became more standardized, there appears to be no special reason to dispute.[49]

In conclusion, our supposition is that -*ariu* turned to -*aru*; that -*aru* absorbed -*ĕriu*, -*ēriu* (or that, after -*ĕriu* had absorbed -*ēriu* and lost its i, the two forms, -*aru* and -*ęru*, coincided by reason of the normal French change of $a < e$, occurring while original $ĕ$ still remained undiphthongized); and that the new -*eru*, with open e, passed on to -*ier* by confusion with $ę < ĕ$. As for Provençal forms in -*er*, -*ier*, -*eir*, they may be taken as borrowings from the neighboring French districts, in which the diphthongization tendency appears to have been strongest; true Provençal development from -*ariu* > -*aru* > -*ar* being represented by forms like *bacalar*, *bachalar*, *cavalar*, and by *clara*, *glara* (< *glarea*), which has no counterpart in *e*, *ie* or *ei*.

A special word is in order concerning the *el* (:*miel*, *Léger*, 102), *eil* (:*mener:plurer:consirrer:aturnet*, *Alexis*, 49; manuscripts other than the Lambspringe have *el*), *el* (*Roland*, CCXLIV, not in assonance; XCII, CCXI, in $e < a$ assonance). This form, which should have come from *aliud*, vulgarized to *alium, is, because of its development, derived from *ale. It is true that a Latin *alis*, *alid* exists; its survival, however, is doubtful. Could *el* indicate a development from *aliu* with fall of i, in contrast with French *ail* < *alium*? If so, the contrast between *premer, *premier* < *primariu* and *vair* < *variu* would have, if not an explanation, at least a parallel.

The Romanic Review, XXXI (1940)

---

[49] For hesitation in the matter of diphthongization in widely different languages and periods, cf. Salverda de Grave, *Neophilologus*, XI (1936), 262.

VII

LATIN AND ITALIAN FINAL FRONT VOWELS

The outcome of Latin final -ī in Italian lends itself to no discussion. Such is not the case, however, with Latin final -ĕ, -ē, -ĭ and the dipththong -ae. Meyer-Lübke [1] suggests that while Latin -ĕ, -ĭ, and -ae became -e in Italian, Latin -ē may have acquired a closer and closer sound until it eventually coincided with Latin -ī; this, in his opinion, would account for the fact that while we have *bene, sette, lume, amasse, piante, ove, crede, forse,* from forms which in Latin had final -ĕ, -ĭ or -ae, we also have *vedi, oggi, lungi,* etc., from forms with an original -ē. In a later work, [2] however, he appears to have modified his opinion, accepting the hypothesis that the outcome of all four Latin vowel sounds in the final syllable is -e, and explaining *dodici* as due to the influence of the preceding *i*; *dieci* as based on the analogy of *venti*; *amassi* (first person) by analogy with *dissi*; *ieri* as derived from an archaic *herī*; *oggi, avanti, anzi, quasi* as due to the influx of the initial vowel of the following word; *ivi* by analogy with *quivi*; *parimenti* with the ending of the second half made to conform with the ending of the first half; then *altrimenti* by analogy with *parimenti*; etc.

This point of view is accepted by Grandgent, [3] who adds to the list of doubtful forms offered by his predecessor *onni* and *ogni*, as due to use before words beginning with vowels; *pari* as derived from

---

[1] *Grammaire des langues romanes* (trad. Rabiet, 1890), I, 306.
[2] D'Ovidio & Meyer-Lübke, *Grammatica storica della lingua e dei dialetti italiani* (trad. Polcari, Milano, 1906), pp. 90-91.
[3] *From Latin to Italian* (Cambridge, 1927), pp. 51-52.

parimenti; *vi* (< *ibĭ*) as due to proclitic use; *assai* (< *ad satĭs*) as influenced by *magis*, which becomes *mai*; *quasi, fuori, ieri* as derived from archaic Latin *quasei, forīs, herī*. He further asserts that at a certain point in linguistic development the *-i* ending acquires the value of a characteristic adverbial termination, thus explaining, at one stroke, *domani, anzi, anti, avanti, tardi, volentieri*, etc.; for the forms of the present subjunctive, such as *ami*,[4] he asserts that the phonological *ame* of the older tongue turns into *ami* at a period when there still was, in the second person singular, among the three endings *-a, -e, -i*, a conflict which ultimately ended in the triumph of the *-i* ending, which served to differentiate the second person from the others.[5] Elsewhere,[6] Grandgent restates his theory to the effect that *-e* is the only truly phonological outcome of the four Latin vocalic sounds in the final syllable, and, opposing the older theories of Meyer-Lübke, cites Vulgar Latin forms such as *verae* to prove that *-ē* shows no signs of coalescing with *-ī*. The *volentieri* which D'Ovidio and Meyer-Lübke attribute to a French influx is expained by Grandgent, together with *domani* and *tardi*, as due to a series of analogical phenomena arising from *oggi* and *ieri*, which are in turn said to be under the influence of *dì* or of the archaic Latin forms *herī* and *manī*.

How acceptable are these theories? The Italian forms in which *-i* appears as the continuator of Latin *-ĕ, -ē, -ĭ, -ae* in the final syllable are extremely numerous and varied, and the explanations offered, based on an entire series of doubtful analogies, leave a question in our minds. If, in addition, we examine the oldest documents of the Italian language, our doubts become still graver.

We deliberately leave aside the *fini* (< *finēs*) of the various tenth-century testimonial formulas of Monte Cassino, Teano and Sessa,[7] concerning which doubts might arise because of the final *-s*, and which would in any case tend to support Meyer-Lübke's original theory. We also leave aside the imperative *trai* (< *trahĕ*)

---

[4] *Op. cit.*, p. 158.

[5] In this connection, D'Ovidio and Meyer-Lübke prefer derivation of all subjunctive forms in *-i* from the second person singular.

[6] *Mélanges Thomas*, pp. 187-193.

[7] Monaci, *Crestomazia italiana dei primi secoli* (Città di Castello, 1912), pp. 1, 523; Monteverdi, *Testi volgari italiani anteriori al Duecento* (Roma, 1935), pp. 13-18.

of the eleventh-century Roman inscription in the Church of San Clemente,[8] since it might be attributed to an analogical influence from the second person singular of the present indicative. The Umbrian Confession Formula[9] of the end of the eleventh century offers us, on the one hand, *ore* in the second person singular of the present subjunctive (*e pregonde te, sacerdote, ke nd'ore pro me*); in other words, *-e*, not *-i*, < *-ēs*. On the other hand it shows us a form *farai* in the third person singular; a most interesting form, which indicates an *-i*, not an *-e* outcome for Latin *-ĕt*. In his discussion[10] of the linguistic features of this ancient text, Flechia expressed himself in the following terms: "*Alti*, errore di scrittura per *altri*, come anche *farai* per *farà*, confuso col *farai* precedente, se già non si fosse foneticamente svolto da *farae*." Flechia too seems to have had the idea that the phonological outcome of Latin *-ĕt* might be or might have been transformed into *-i*. In the same formula we also find *ui* (< *aut*, > *o, oe*) repeated twice.

In contrast with the final *-i* of the Formula, we find the forms *fue, sagroe, destinoe, peroe* of the *Ritmo giullaresco toscano*[11] of the second half of the twelfth century.[12]

A document from Fabriano of the year 1186[13] has the form *teni* in the third person singular; it may be objected, however, that we are drawing somewhat too far away from the Central Italian region.

The *Dichiarazione pistojese* of 1195[14] shows us *fue, aguale, concioe, arcipreite*, with final *-e*; but also *nanti*, repeated four times, and never before a vowel, as D'Ovidio and Meyer-Lübke suppose, nor, presumably, at the period when final *-i* had already become a characteristic adverbial ending, as Grandgent holds.

The twelfth-century *Ritmo marchigiano di Sant' Alessio*[15] shows

---

[8] Monaci, p. 4; Monteverdi, p. 26.
[9] Monaci, p. 5; Monteverdi, pp. 26-29.
[10] *Archivio glottologico italiano*, VII, p. 129.
[11] Monaci, p. 9; Monteverdi, pp. 29-31.
[12] The form *stenetietti*, glossed by Monaci 'abstieni e tienti', contains a *te* > *ti* which I do not want to discuss here because it involves the difficult question of the atonic personal pronouns.
[13] Monaci, p. 11; Monteverdi, pp. 49-51.
[14] Monteverdi, p. 62.
[15] Monteverdi, pp. 71-80; his readings have been used in preference to those of Monaci, which show, however, very slight deviation.

a remarkable interchange of -*e* and -*i*; *foe* (line 15) followed by *foi* in the next line; *onni die* (35) as against *onne iurnu* (50); *fae* (92, 113) as against *stai* (97) and *vai* (98, 242) in the third person; *poi* (81) in contrast with *poe* (107); *mai* (111, 194) and *mae* (180); *noe* for *no, non* (110); and even *lue* (187) for *lui*. It may be objected that we are too far away from the Central Italian zone; but even so, the appearance of definite fluctuation in what was later to become a dialect is circumstantial evidence for the same possibility in what was later to become the literary tongue.

Passing on to the thirteenth century, we take from the *Biblioteca capitolare di Lucca* [16] that fragment of the third chapter of the *Regola di San Benedetto* which is entitled *De Adhibendis ad Consilium Fratribus Expositio,* which has the advantage of having, side by side with the Italian version, the Latin translation. Here we find: *dici* for *dice*; *fari* for *fare*; *utili* for *utile*; *conueni* for *conviene*; *obediri*; *matamenti*; *tuti cosse*; *esseri*; all this, along with numerous forms having final -*e*; *labate, humeltate, defendere, rumore, paresse, utille, providere, iustamente, tute le cosse, sequitare, uoluntate,* etc.

Furthermore, and this is quite extraordinary, we find the repetition of the Umbrian phenomenon of the ending -*ai* in the third person singular of the future: *iudicarai,* repeated twice (the Latin version has *iudicaverit*).

Lastly, a document from Pistoja of the year 1259 [17] shows the occurrence of *eredi* twice in the singular, and of *innanthi* once before a consonant (*innanthi saldemo*).

The conclusion seems fairly clear. From the very first appearance of Italian texts, there is in evidence a conflict between -*e* and -*i* to occupy the place of the four Latin vowel sounds, -$\breve{e}$, -$\bar{e}$, -$\breve{\iota}$, -*ae* in the final syllable, and this conflict persists to our own times. The double forms appearing in the same text are incontrovertible evidence of this conflict. Nor does it avail Grandgent to say [18] that a more or less paragogic -*e* is added to words ending in an accented

---

[16] Cod. 93, f. 18v and 19.
[17] Monaci, p. 160.
[18] *Op. cit.,* p. 48. Cf. also, in this connection, Hall, *Language,* xv (1939), pp. 224-228 and *Italica,* xvii (1940), pp. 123-124; and Shaw *Italica,* xvii (1940), pp. 78-79.

vowel (for some of the monosyllabic forms cited, such as *ui, vai, stai, noe,* and for the *peroe* of the *Ritmo giullaresco,* the vowel seems definitely paragogic; for other forms, such as *farai, fue* or *fui, fae, iudicarai,* one may object that the vowel is not paragogic, but the continuator of the Latin final vowel). At any rate, the "paragogic" vowel obeys the same "law of fluctuation" as the original final vowel; it wavers between *-e* and *-i.*

What can be the cause of this apparent phonological fluctuation? Can it be altogether ascribed to dialectal or "learned" influences, or to scribal "error"? Or is it a survival of a similar fluctuation appearing, in the case of several words, in archaic and even in Classical Latin?[19] Or is it a new wavering that arises, in the formative period of Italian, by reason of indistinct pronunciation in the final syllable brought about by heavy stress-accent in the tonic syllable, and which later gives way to normalized orthography and pronunciation as the language becomes literary?

If one of the last two possibilities is at the root of the phenomena we have described, then it is possible that a clue is finally offered for the solution of the much-discussed problem of Italian third-declension plurals (*cani* < *canēs*),[20] as well as, at least in part, of the other vexing problem of the second person singular endings of the verb (*vedi* < *vidēs; reggi* < *regĭs; dormi* < *dormīs;* then, by an analogical process far more restricted than the one claimed by Grandgent, *ami* replacing *ama* < *amās*). In view of the fluctuation in the outcome of Latin *-ĕ, -ē, -ĭ, -ae* in the final syllable, it does not seem unreasonable to suppose that Italian speakers may have made use of the two possibilities to establish a distinction

---

[19] *Quasĭ-quasei; ibĭ-ibī (Aeneid,* ii, 792); *herĭ-herī* (Ovid, *Fasti,* ii, 76); *ubĭ-ube-ubei-ubīque;* cf. Sommer, *Handbuch der lat. Laut- und Formenlehre,*[2] 149-150; Diehl, *Vulgärlateinische Inschriften,* 226-*merente;* 337-*abis;* 1307-*valis.*

[20] For another explanation of *cani* < *canēs* (that Italian *-i* is the survival of a Latin older third-declension accusative *-īs*), cf. Puşcariu, *Mélanges Thomas,* pp. 359-365; Pei, *The Italian Language* (New York, 1941), p. 73. For the available textual evidence from the Vulgar Latin period in connection with this explanation, cf. Pei, *The Language of the Eighth-Century Texts in Northern France* (New York, 1932), pp. 147-150, and references listed therein. While this explanation may be acceptable for the plural of third-declension nouns, it contributes nothing to the solution of the problem of the *-i* in the second person singular of verbs.

between *cane* singular and *cani* plural (with, perhaps, some analogical help from the model of the Latin second-declension plural in -*ī*), and between *vede* and *regge* in the third person and *vedi* and *reggi* in the second.

Modern Language Notes, LVIII (1943)

VIII

INTERVOCALIC OCCLUSIVES IN "EAST" AND "WEST" ROMANCE

While the idea of a cleavage between the East and the West of the Romance domain is not new, considerable uncertainty reigned in the minds of earlier linguists concerning its precise nature. Geographical and historical factors lent themselves to his confusion. On the one hand, Dacia, permanently severed from communication with the rest of Romania in the Sixth Century, presented an ideal possibility of linguistic cleavage, with isolated Roumanian left standing in opposition to the rest of the Romance languages with their territorial contiguity; this opposition appeared strengthened by certain linguistic phenomena (post-posed article, conservation of certain elements of the Latin declensional scheme, and of segments of the Classical phonology and vocabulary, Slavic instead of Germanic lexical innovations, etc.). On the other hand, the eastern position of Italy with respect to Gaul and Iberia, the barrier of the Alps, the existence of a former Latin bridgehead across the Adriatic in the form of the provinces of Moesia and Illyricum, coupled with other linguistic factors (fall of final -s, noun plurals from what seems to be the nominative rather than the accusative or the oblique, partial retention of intervocalic consonants in their original form) led to the rather indefinite formulation of an Italian-Roumanian "East" as opposed to a Franco-Hispanic "West". [1]

---

[1] Typical of this somewhat confused state of mind, to cite but one instance, is Bourciez, (*Eléments de linguistique romane,* Paris, 1930), who seemingly uses "Orient" and "Occident" to distinguish between Dacia and the

It remained for the linguists of the present generation to come to a precise definition of the nature and causes of the supposed cleavage, localizing it in time and space. W. von Wartburg is the pioneer in this field. In his article *Die Ausgliederung der romanischen Sprachräume*,[2] he offers a painstaking analysis of the facts which lead him to postulate a fundamental linguistic unity between Roumania and Italy south of a line running from Spezia to Rimini, as against another fundamental unity embracing northern Italy, Gaul and Iberia, with some fluctuation on the part of Sardinia and Corsica. This linguistic cleavage is accepted in its entirety (though its causes are not) by G. Devoto,[3] and is restated, in the form of a phonological law, without any discussion as to causes, by R. A. Hall, Jr.[4]

Von Wartburg's contention is the following: East and West Romance are distinguished by two fundamental phonological differences, the fall vs. the retention of final *-s*, and the conservation vs. the sonorization and fall of intervocalic occlusives. Other factors brought into the discussion, but discarded (page 15), because they do not coincide with the geographical line of the cleavage, are the change of *-ct-* to *-χt, -it-,* vs. its retrogressive assimilation to *-tt-* or change to *-pt-,* and the change of $\bar{u}$ to $\ddot{u}$ vs. its retention. The Spezia-Rimini line is chosen because to the north of it both late retention of final *-s* and sonorization and fall of intervocalic occlusives appear.

Von Wartburg is definite in his rejection of substratum influences in the development of at least one of his two fundamental differences. He states (page 4) that Gaulish inscriptions show frequent fall of final *-s*, and his explanation is that whereas Dacia was

---

rest of the Romance world, "Est" and "Ouest" to differentiate between Dacia and Italy on the one hand and the remaining Romance countries on the other. Speaking of the article (227c) he says, "En Orient fut préféré dès le début l'ordre *homo ille*" (cf. also 228a, 237, 213a, for the survival of a specific dative case); but in the matter of proparoxytonic retention (152a) he says, "sur ce point, les langues de l'Est (italien, roumain) s'opposent assez nettement à celles de l'Ouest (espagnol, provençal, français)"; and in discussing intervocalic consonants ('171), "l'Est du domaine roman s'oppose ici à l'Ouest d'une façon très nette".

[2] *ZRP* LVI (1936), 1-49. His position is restated in his *Posizione della lingua italiana*, Firenze, 1940.

[3] *Storia della lingua di Roma*, Bologna, 1940.

[4] Review of Pei, *The Italian Language, Language,* XVII, 3 (1941), 263-269.

practically depopulated of its original inhabitants and resettled by rough Roman soldiers and colonists who brought with them the "rustic" Italian habit of dropping final -s, Gaul and Iberia were somewhat aristocratically latinized by means of towns, schools, state officials and the upper ranks of society. One is tempted to wonder why these conservative influences should have worked only in favor of final -s, and not in favor of intervocalic occlusives, -ct-, and ū. What was the social and cultural background of northern Italy which led it to join distant and aristocratic Gaul and Iberia rather than the supposedly more untutored but geographically closer center and south of Italy? The author does not enlighten us. A minor weakness in his demonstration is that in his eagerness to prove West Romance conditions and the late retention of final -s north of the Spezia-Rimini line, he uses as evidence not only cases of real survival appearing in ancient texts and present-day dialects, but also forms indicating the *fall* of -s (*le stela*)[5] and feminine plural forms in -i appearing in thirteenth-century Bologna documents (*carti, chaxi*), which, he says, must come from *chartas, capsas* (why not from dative-ablative *chartis, capsis*, with normal fall of final -s?).

Devoto (page 296), approaching the problem from his classicist's background accepts von Wartburg's Spezia-Rimini line *in toto*, but postulates entirely different reasons: the geographical border of the Appennines, the ethnical border, with a former Celtic-speaking region to the north of the line, and substitution of an east-west arrangement of roads for the former north-south network. The first of these reasons leads us to wonder why the Alps could not have served far more effectively than the Appennines as a linguistic frontier; if the Appennines did so serve, why does their effectiveness end at the Adriatic coast instead of being carried down into central and southern Italy? The second is the substratum argument which von Wartburg wisely avoids; Venetia and Friuli, north of the line,

---

[5] This, he says, indicates derivation from *stellas*, not from *stellae*. Granted. But does this necessarily prove late fall of final -s in *stellas*? The dialect in question may not have felt the need for a distinction between singular and plural, since the article supplied that distinction, much as modern spoken French does not feel the need for a distinction between *étoile* and *étoiles*, which the article supplies. Furthermore, the article *le* in *le stela* indicates a mixture of forms and derivations which von Wartburg does not take into account.

do not have a Celtic substratum; yet they share with the rest of the north and with Gaul the tendency to retain final -*s* and sonorize intervocalic surds. The last point is something which Devoto does not at all conclusively prove, and for which the services of historians rather than linguists are needed; but if the east-west road axis should prove true, it would nevertheless be in conflict with Italian-Roumanian unity, for both it and the Spezia-Rimini line tend to break all territorial continuity and land lines of communication between centro-southern Italy and Dacia, leaving nothing but overseas contact, unsatisfactory at best, as admitted by Devoto himself (page 299).

Hall, while submitting no element of evidence or causation, and concentrating upon only one of von Wartburg's two fundamental linguistic features, is perhaps the most rigid assertor of the cleavage between East and West Romance. He formulates the "law" with respect to intervocalic occlusives (p. 264): "...the cleavage between East and West Romance in what might well be called the 'West Romance sound-shift' of intervocalic occlusives (double unvoiced > single unvoiced; single unvoiced > single voiced; single voiced drops)"; and he goes on to claim the prevalence of East Romance conditions in this respect in Tuscany and of West Romance conditions in northern Italy, with "the consequent conclusion" (p. 265) "that words showing the West Romance sound-shift (*strada, madre, riva, pagare*) are borrowings from North Italian or other West Romance dialects".

The situation, in summary, is the following: a definite linguistic cleavage between "East Romance" (Roumanian, "Dalmatian", south and central Italian) and "West Romance" (North Italian, including both Venetian and Gallo-Italian groups, Rhaetian, French, Provençal, Spanish and Portuguese) is claimed by followers of the von Wartburg-Devoto-Hall school; they are not at all agreed as to the time when the cleavage occurred,[6] or as to its causes; they base

---

[6] Von Wartburg sets no definite date or century, but it is evident from his discussion that he places it no later than Trajan's Dacian conquest; while Devoto, claiming substantial linguistic unity throughout the Latin world down to the time of Diocletian (pages 281-282), places it after the beginning of the fourth century. Hall's point of view as to the reduction of double consonants and the chronology of the Spezia-Rimini line is not stated in the above-mentioned review. but transpires from a subsequent article ("Latin

their conclusions upon two phonological phenomena, disregarding numerous other traits, phonological, morphological, syntactical and lexical, in which one of the "Eastern" languages (but not the others) coincides with the "West", or vice-versa; these fundamental phenomena are: 1. the fall of final -*s*, with consequent plural formation from the nominative in East Romance, as against conservation of final -*s* and plural formation from accusative or oblique in West Romance; 2. Hall's above-stated law for the shift of intervocalic occlusives in West Romance, as against their conservation in East Romance.

The first of these two differences seems the more obvious and undeniable, though the questions of chronology and geographical distribution appear far from solved. Whether in itself fall or retention of -*s*, even with its morphological consequences, suffices to permit us to speak of a linguistic cleavage is something which may depend upon individual taste. Fall of other final consonants, which did not involve morphological structure, the treatment of stressed vowels, or of final vowels, the retention of a pluri-case systen *vs.* the complete simplification of the Latin declensional scheme, the use of *ille vs. ipse* as a definite article, or of a prefixed *vs.* a post-posed article, retention of *-ui* and *-orum* pronominal forms *vs.* retention of *-ujus* forms, or any other of a large number of phonological or morphological factors could as well be selected as the basis for cleavage into separate Romance groups. Perhaps the morphological result of the fall of final -*s* has been allowed to assume a paramount importance in the minds of "East and West Romance" believers, instead of being placed in its proper perspective. But if the Italian and Roumanian plural derived from the Latin nominative is made the basis for Italian-Roumanian unity, ought not the single case of

---

-*ks*- in Italian", *Language*, XVIII, 2 [April-June 1942], 117-124. Here he shows page 119) a series of maps which indicate the -*ss*- outcome, "by the beginning of the Middle Ages", in an area including all of Italy except Piedmont, Liguria, and western Lombardy, then reduction of double *s* to single *s* in northeastern Italy (Venetia, Emilia, eastern Lombardy), by the "Old Italian Period". He finishes by stating (page 122) that the northern limit of -*ss*- runs along the Spezia-Rimini line, "as do a great number of isoglosses separating northern Italy from central and southern Italy". If the reduction of double *s* to single *s* is at all significant in connection with the Spezia-Rimini line, the establishment of the latter presumably had not yet occurred "by the early Middle Ages" and became a reality only in the "Old Italian Period".

Italian, Spanish and Portuguese *vs.* the double case of French and Provençal and the vestiges of a pluri-case system in Roumanian to be made the basis for a hypothetical Italian-Iberian unity? A single phonological phenomenon, even though it be morphologically fruitful, in which two linguistic groups coincide does not necessarily establish a fundamental unity between those groups. [7]

The second divergence between East and West Romance is perhaps more fundamental if it can be truly established, since it represents not a single, isolated phenomenon (however important in far-reaching morphological results), but a general phonological trend affecting an entire class of sounds. Here we must scrutinize Hall's definitely formulated phonological law and the "West Romance sound-shift." If the law has been properly formulated, forms showing retention of Latin double occlusives, intervocalic surds and intervocalic sonants in the Iberian peninsula, France, Rhaetia and Italy north of the Spezia-Rimini line must be proved to be of learned or imported origin; similarly, Italian forms south of the line and Roumanian and Vegliote forms in general which show simplification, sonorization or fall of intervocalic occlusives must be proved to be, as Hall states, "borrowings from a West Romance dialect".

While the law holds in general for the West Romance group, [8]

---

[7] Note the complete coincidence in the matter of palatalization of gutturals between Italian and Picard, an otherwise typically French dialect, geographically separated from Italy; Italian coincidence with French in the diphthongization of $\breve{e}$ and $\breve{o}$, free and checked, (though non-diphthongizing Provençal intervenes), but with Spanish in connection with $\bar{e}$ and $\bar{o}$ (though there is no geographical contiguity); the coincidence, at least in the initial stage, of Italian and Spanish in the palatalizing of initial *pl, cl, fl* groups, as against the conservatism of intervening French, Provençal and Rhaetian. The fact seems to be that phonological or morphological coincidences between two or more Romance groups, contiguous or separated, are numerous, and that they are not necessarily to be interpreted as establishing any kind of specific linguistic unity between the groups in which they occur. It is interesting in this connection to note that Italian and Roumanian have the same formula for the palatalization of gutturals ($c > \check{c}$ before *e, i*), a fact which was overlooked by von Wartburg in his demonstration; but lest he derive too much comfort from it, it may also be pointed out that Vegliote, the survivor of the "Dalmatian" or "Illyrian" Vulgar Latin which must once have formed the connecting link between Italy and Dacia, retains gutturals generally before *e* and sometimes before *i*.

[8] Outside of conservative forms which appear to be learned, we have such forms as Sp. *sepa, quepa, coto, hoto, sauco,* and some similar forms in

its working is by no means uniform for all sections, but displays interesting differences of degree. "Double unvoiced > single unvoiced" appears generally in modern times. What may be the significance of the numerous double-consonant spellings of the West Romance tongues in their earlier stages is a matter of conjecture. It may well be that the frequent use of double consonants in Old French, Old Spanish and Old Portuguese represents nothing but a learned restoration or an orthographical device. But are we altogether certain? [9]

"Single unvoiced > single voiced" is normally true of Spanish, Portuguese, Provençal and north Italian (though the "single voiced" often passes from a plosive to a fricative; Sp. *amada, amiga, saber*, where the apparent sonant plosives really have the value of fricatives); in French the process generally goes further, to the complete fall of the single unvoiced (*amata > amede > aimée, amica > amie*; note also Sp. *amades > amáis* and popular Sp. *amado > amao*).

Portuguese and Provençal, but the cònservation of the surd may perhaps be explained as due to the influx of a diphthong; cf. Meyer-Lübke, *Grammaire des languages romanes*, I, 434; for the retention of Latin surds and sonants in a few western varieties of Provençal, cf. Bourciez, *op. cit.*, 171b, 270a.

[9] The Spanish Glosses of Silos offer such forms as *adduitos* and *occisiones*; *vaccas* appears in a Leonese document of 1002, *offeyro* in a Portuguese document of 1193. Rhaetian (Obwald and Engadine) religious works of the late sixteenth and early seventeenth centuries have *puccaus, peccadurs, bucca, inguotta*. Perhaps the most striking cases of double consonants, by reason of implications and later results, are the ones appearing in France: the *Eulalie's getterent* indicates a retrogressive assimilation of *-ct-* to *-tt-*, only later simplified to *-t-*; still more important is the form *tottus*, criticized by Consentius in the fifth century, reappearing (*tutti*) in the Glosses of Cassel and (*tuttum*) in a Merovingian eighth century charter, and ultimately giving rise to Mod. Fr. *tout*, which must come from *tŭttu* or *tōttu*, not from *tōtu*; here documentary evidence combines with historical development to indicate the existence of a gemination tendency on West Romance soil, with conservation and even creation of double consonants extending far beyond any hypothetical date of division between East and West Romance. Outside of the occlusive field, this geminative tendency is also attested by frequent *-mmus* spellings for the first person plural of the present and perfect (cf. Pei, *The Language of the Eighth-Century Texts in Northern France*, N. Y., 1932, pages 113-117), the phonetic reality of which is proved by *sommes* < *summus*, not < *sumus*; *amames* < *amammus*, not < *ama(vi)mus*, etc. Reference could likewise be made to forms like *gyppus, sappas* in the Glosses of Cassel and *quaccòla* in the Glosses of Reichenau, along with what may be interpreted as traditional spellings, such as *lippus, beccus, promittere, bucca, sagittarum, gutture, reddita*, etc.

"Single voiced drops" frequently fails to operate (Prov. *plaga, vezer, fava*; Fr. *fève*; Sp. *suda, llaga* vs. *coa, lía*; Pt. *legar, chaga* vs. *eu, liar, lidar, estria*). The state of affairs throughout indicates a general tendency in the direction of the formulated "law", with cases of resistance, often carried by one language through an entire series, and other cases in which one tongue carries the tendency through beyond the goal described by the law.

When we come to the "East Romance" group, the situation is more interesting. Here, presumably, none of the phenomena of the "West Romance sound-shift" should be operative, and forms which obey the sound-shift law should be proved to be of borrowed origin. [10]

Easternmost Roumanian, which might be expected to display the most extreme conservatism in the matter of intervocalic occlusives, shows, on the contrary, complete agreement with the western languages for what concerns double occlusives. These are invariably simplified (*gutta* > *gută, cuppa* > *cupă, bucca* > *bucă*, etc.), and this state of affairs goes back to the earliest appearance of Roumanian documents in the sixteenth century. Intervocalic surds are not sonorized; dental and guttural sonants are not dropped, but labial sonants are (*caballu* > *cal, scribo* > *scriu, lavare* > *la*; note also *detoriile* < *debitores illi*—Lord's Prayer of Luca Stroicǐ, 1593; *oile* < *oves illae*—Cazania of Varlaam, 1643). The coincidence of Roumanian with the ideal East Romance state of affairs is therefore far from complete.

Vegliote, the supposed descendant of "Dalmatian" or "Illyrian" Vulgar Latin, the connection (with a watery break) between the language of Dacia and that of Italy south of the Spezia-Rimini line, shows a state of affairs very similar to that of Roumanian. Double occlusives are simplified in accordance with the "West Romance" sound-shift (*bucca* > *buka*), while single surds are retained unsonorized and single sonants are not dropped, in accordance with the "East Romance" system (*spuota, struota, raipa* < *spatha, strata, ripa*; *cotidiun, debete* < *cotidianu, debita*).

---

[10] The "learned" factor, which is invoked in the case of West Romance retention of Latin double occlusives, single surds and single sonants, is, of course, out of the question here.

For centro-southern Italy, a complete historical picture can be presented, running from Latin inscriptional material through Vulgar Latin texts and early Italian documents to the present-day Linguistic Atlas.

Unlike the other "eastern" languages, (Roumanian, Vegliote), centro-southern Italian retains Latin double occlusives and has a strong tendency to geminate (*brutto, acqua, cappone, appo, febbre*). In this area we find the victorious counterpart of the abortive geminative tendency of Gaul leading to French *tout* and *sommes* (*tutto*, Basilicatan *amammo* < *amamus*, Neapolitan *iammo* < *eamus*, etc.). It may be said that centro-southern Italian, in this respect, not only obeys the "law" postulated for the East Romance languages (double occlusives stay), but is the *only* East Romance language to do so.

In the matter of conservation of single surd and sonant occlusives, where the other East Romance groups display complete or almost complete conservatism, centro-southern Italian shows extremely mixed results. Sonorization of intervocalic single surds, while far from universal, is very common; fall of sonants occasional. Is it possible that all forms showing sonorization of surds and fall of sonants are "borrowings from North Italian or other West Romance dialects"? Such forms are extremely numerous and extremely popular; they appear not only in the literary tongue, but in the dialects as well; they are not merely modern, but run back to the Latin inscriptions and through the pre-Italian Latin texts of central and southern Italy.

Von Wartburg claims (*op. cit.*, page 8) that the inscriptions show evidence of no sonorization of intervocalic surds south of the Spezia-Rimini line. No special attempt has been made by the present writer to collect examples of inscriptions displaying such sonorization in the centro-southern Italian zone (such a study might prove of interest), but using and verifying only cases cited in existing manuals, we find: CIL IV 1486 (Pompei) — *pagatus*; VI 12944 (Rome) — *Amadus*; VI 15471 (Rome) — *fegit*; X 4528 (Capua) — *agolitus*; XIV 3571 (Tibur) — *sagrum*.

Schiaparelli, *Codice diplomatico longobardo* (Roma, 1929) shows

numerous cases of sonorization in central Italian (Tuscan) eighth-century documents, of which the following are samples: [11]
Lucca, 700 (page 31) — *eglesie* (*ecclesie* on same page); (page 32) — *sagrosancto*. Siena, 715 (page 69) — *consagrationem, Lubercianus, Aredine, sagratus*; *sagrati*; (page 72) — *sagramenta, Aredine* (*Aretine* on same page); page 74 — *madodinos*; (page 75) — *probe, oradorius*. San Pietro in Neure, 716 (page 86) — *aeglesias, eglesia*; (page 87) — *degreuimus, iudegati, sagramentus*.

A brief Abruzzian text of the year 819 (*Bullettino dell'Istituto Storico Italiano*, no. 45) shows the following sonorized forms: *liver* (for *liber*, with sonant plosive > sonant spirant); *sagrosanctu*; *sicut ed alis monachi* (with *et* becoming *ed* by reason of intervocalic position).

Coming down to the earliest centro-southern texts, we find: Monteverdi, *Testi volgari italiani* (Roma, 1935) — page 27 (Umbria, 11th century) — *aulteria, dei* (for *diedi*), *pregonde*; page 62 (Pistoia, 1195) — *aguale, vescovo*. Monaci, *Crestomazia italiana dei primi secoli* (Città di Castello, 1912) — page 9 (Tuscany, 12th century) — *sagrato, sovrano*; page 19 (Florence, 1211) — *pagare*; page 160 (Pistoia, 1259) — *lire*; page 462 (Perugia, 13th century) — *pregamo, priegal, pieje* (for *piedi*), *nero*; page 36 (Siena, 13th century) — *Moschada, livre*; page 548 (Otranto, 15th century) — *luegy* (as against *lueco*). Schiaffini, *Testi fiorentini del Dugento*, XXVIII: "Si sa che *fatiga* o *fadiga* è dei dialetti toscani occidentali e meridionali"; *pogo, segondo, seguro, regare, avogado, fuogo, figo* (Dante), *miga* (Boccaccio) are among the forms cited as examples. Other sonorized forms in Schiaffini's collection (Glossary, s. v.) are: *medesimo, parladore, raunare*. Papanti, *I Parlari italiani a Certaldo* (Firenze, 1875; nineteenth-century dialectal translations

---

[11] The possibility that scribes from northern Italy may have been the composers of these Tuscan documents from the Longobardic period must, of course, be reckoned with. Placed in relation with earlier inscriptional material and later Italian texts, however, these forms seem to point to the continuation of an already existing tendency to sonorization. A basis of comparison is perhaps supplied by other documents in the same collection from northern Italy, in which cases of sonorization are far more abundant (Campione, 735, page 176) — *rogadus, pedidus, secudi, fenidum, interposido, tradida*; Trevano, 748, page 274 — *udilitatibus, prado, capide, rio, dublo*; Asti, 754, page 357 — *finido, mesuaradas, dublis, reddeduri, meliurada, terredurio, nebodes, probria, rogidus, tradida*).

of Boccaccio) gives us the following sonorized forms from the south: *preio* (Nola); *fatia* (Salerno); *sceze* (Melfi); *fatiia* (Matera); *digghe* (for *dico* — Bari).

Jaberg & Jud, *Sprach- und Sachatlas Italiens und der Südschweiz* (Zofingen, 1928) shows *padre,* not *patre,* in universal use throughout Tuscany, Marche, Umbria, northern Latium, northern Abruzzi, while *madre,* not *matre,* appears in all Tuscany, Marche and northern Latium; *marito* appears as *marido* in Marche, Umbria, northern Abruzzi, Latium and Bari; the same regions use *cognado, cognada, cognadi* for *cognato, cognata, cognati* (Colli goes as far as *suo goñado*); *magro* appears in Tuscany, Umbria, Marche, Latium, Abruzzi, Calabria, Sicily; *catena* is rendered as *cadena* all along the Adriatic coast, from Marche to the tip of Puglia; *fuogo* replaces *fuoco* in many sections of Umbria, Latium, Marche and Abruzzi; *formiga* replaces *formica* in most of Marche, Umbria, northern Latium, northern Abruzzi; *lagrima* predominates in Marche, Umbria, southern Tuscany, northern Latium, northern Abruzzi, sections of Puglia, Calabria, Campania, Basilicata and Sicily; *pregare* shows a sonorized form or complete fall of the original surd guttural practically everywhere; *padella* < *patella* appears in Marche, Abruzzi, Tuscany, most of Latium, Calabria and Sicily. This list could be greatly extended, and borrowing from the literary language, which might be tentatively advanced for forms like *magro, lagrima, pregare* and *padella,* is out of the question for *marido, cognado, formiga, cadena,* etc.

This confused state of affairs with respect to sonorization in centro-southern Italian, with the appearance of a definite tendency to sonorize coupled with an equally definite resistance to sonorization in the identical area, is fully recognized in existing manuals, the authors of which appear torn between the desire to generalize and set up stringent phonological "laws" and the necessity of admitting linguistic facts as they are actually recorded.

Meyer-Lübke, *Grammaire des langues romanes,* I (Paris, 1890-1906), endeavoring to find a "phonologically legal" formula for the altogether too numerous cases of sonorization of intervocalic occlusives in Italian, informs us (433-434) that surd plosives following the accent are sonorized before *a* (*strada, spada, paga, piega, bottega, priva,* etc.); forms like *luogo, ago, lago, scudo, grado, -tade,* etc. are explained by a series of slightly questionable analogies and dissimilations; the guttural sonant is described (438) as falling in Sicily and Taranto (*rua, fau, lia* < *ruga, fagu, legat*), as passing to i̯ in Teramo and Abruzzi (*maiə* < *fagu*): *v*, original or coming from *b*, is described (442) as falling in the south-eastern dialects (Lecce *scriu, via, nue, faa, koa, noe* < *scribo, viva, nube, faba, cubat, novem*); to these, he adds Italian fall of *v* < *b* between two *e*'s (*prete, bere* < *presbyter, bibere*); surd plosives before the accent are described as sonorizing in Italian (443 — *arrivare, cavelli, podere, scodella, padella, pagare*), and he goes so far as to claim fall of intervocalic sonants in that position (*reale, fraore*, etc.), while sonorization is claimed (445) for palatalized *c* (*magella, ugello, dugento*); and fall of *v*, original or from *b*, before back vowels (446 — *paone*, Pisan *auto, riceuto*); lastly, sonorization of *tr* and *cr* after *a* is claimed (494 — *padre, madre, ladro, agro, magro, lagrima, lograre*), together with fall of *g* in the *gr* group irrespective of surrounding vowel sounds (*nero, intero, perezza*), and *pr* > *vr* before the accent (*sovrano*).

Bourciez, *Eléments de linguistique romane* (Paris, 1930), (405), prefers a formula whereby intervocalic surds are sonorized in centro-southern Italian in proparoxytonic forms (*segale, redina, povero*) and preserved elsewhere (*fuoco, sete, capo*), but admits that before the accent *c* passes to *g* (*pagare, dragone, aguglia*); forms such as *lattuga, scudo, strada, riva, padella, arrivare* are labelled as northern loan-words; he grants *cr* > *gr* (*lagrima, segreto*), but *tr* > *dr* only ofter *a* (*padre*, but *pietra*); in all of Umbria, he states, Italian primary or secondary *d* falls (*suore, paella, nio, strae, fracio, trubio*).

Bertoni, *Italia dialettale* (Milano, 1916), page 155, n. 1, after speaking of the general tendency of southern Italian dialects to preserve intervocalic surds, goes on to observe that in Potenza and vicinity there is a sonorization center that may be compared to northern Italy (*savé, avert, prevere, sfugá, affuá*), and concludes: "Se si nota altresì che frequenti esemplari con digradamento guizzano per tutta l'Italia centro-meridionale (p. e. sicil. *arrigurdari*, cal. *pigula*, otrant. *aredu*, Abr. *pajudî*) dobbiamo accettare con qualche riserva codesta norma generale della conservazione delle sorde, se anche non si voglia ammettere che la sorda possa rappresentare in molti casi un ritorno a condizioni primitive per effetto di un fenomeno relativamente moderno."

Whether or not we accept the theories of Meyer-Lübke and Bourciez concerning sonorization and fall of intervocalic occlusives in centro-southern Italian as due to proparoxytonic position or the presence of a specific preceding or following vowel, enough evidence appears to permit us to speak very definitely of a tendency toward sonorization and fall of intervocalic occlusives in that region, a tendency which, while linking centro-southern Italian to the so-called West Romance languages, places it in opposition to "East Romance" Vegliote and Roumanian, with their almost complete conservation of single intervocalic occlusives.[12] The opposition is strengthened by a comparison of centro-southern Italian's tendency to keep double occlusives and to geminate with the "West Romance" lack of gemination and the simplification of Latin double occlusives appearing in Vegliote and Roumanian.

The situation for the entire Romance area with respect to Latin intervocalic occlusives may be summarized as follows:

	Double > single	*Surd > sonant*	*Sonant falls*
Portuguese	normally	normally	normally, with exceptions
Spanish	normally	normally	normally, with exceptions
French	normally, but with occasional doubling	normally and beyond	normally, save for labials
Provençal	normally	normally	normally, with exceptions
Rhaetian	normally	normally	normally, with exceptions
North Italian	normally	normally	normally, with exceptions
Centro-southern Italian	exceptionally, with far more frequent doubling	frequently	frequently
Vegliote	normally	never	never
Roumanian	normally	never	never, save for labials

---

[12] Yet note that in Roumanian this conservation is not absolute, since *b* and *v* fall.

This picture, far from indicating an "East Romance" conservative unity as opposed to a "West Romance" sound-shift, shows Vegliote and Roumanian in complete agreement with the Western tongues in the matter of doubles, with the centro-southern Italian geminative tendency standing by itself, save for disturbing sporadic occurrences appearing especially in the language (French) which carries the remainder of the sound-shift to its furthest limits. In the matter of surds > sonants and sonants fall, it shows almost complete resistance to the trend in Vegliote and Roumanian, with centro-southern Italian occupying an intermediate position, and very disturbing cases of resistance to the trend, especially for the fall of sonants, in the western group, coupled with an equally disturbing fall of labial sonants in easternmost Roumanian. Under the circumstances, it seems more exact to speak of a general Romance trend (doubles > singles; surds > sonants; sonants fall), accompanied by conservative resistance, which attains its maximum in the centro-southern Italian retention of doubles and gemination and in the Vegliote and Roumanian normal retention of single occlusives. French is the tongue carrying this general tendency to its furthest limits, and this is in full accord with northern France's historical position of chronological leadership in Romance linguistic change. But French itself, in its occasional gemination and in its retention of the labial sonant spirant, indicates the existence of a conservative resistance which appears to a far more marked degree, probably by reason of historical and psychological factors, in Italy, Veglia and Roumania.

The Romance group that has been deliberately omitted from the picture given above is Sardinian. Sardinian presents a dilemma to von Wartburg. He admits (page 8, note 3) that the inner dialects of Sardinia retain *p, t, k* unchanged, while the south of the island sonorizes them. Elsewhere (page 16) he appears disturbed by the fact that Sardinian and Corsican join the West in retaining final -*s*, [13] but the East in generally retaining intervocalic occlusives. If the theory of separate East and West Romance groups were correct, it would seem, on the one hand, that there ought to be uniform deve-

---

[13] Has this been proved to be historically true for Corsica and the northern Sardinian dialects (Sassari, Gallura)?

lopment for intervocalic occlusives in this small and comparatively remote area; instead of this we find, from the earliest appearance of Sardinian documents (eleventh century) general sonorization in the southern area, general conservation in the central region; secondly, if the theory were true, we should expect Sardinian to go over as a whole to one or the other of the two systems in both of the major features on which the hypothetical distinction between East and West Romance is based (fall or retention of final -*s*, occlusive soundshift). But even if we grant that north Sardinian (Sassarese, Gallurese) fall of final -*s* is an innovation, we are faced with a "West Romance" conservation of final -*s* in central and southern Sardinian dialects vs. an "Eastern" retention of occlusives in the central part of the island. Sardinian, then, appears to be the meeting-ground of "Eastern" and "Western" tendencies. But while the existence of such a transition zone works very well in favor of the theory of a general Romance trend, with gradually increasing areas of resistance, it does not work at all well for a break between the East and the West, said to have occurred at the time of Trajan or Diocletian.

Simplification and sonorization tendencies are in universal evidence throughout the entire Romance world. Their point of inception is difficult to determine, though the Latin inscriptions offer some clue. That they should go further in some languages than in others is fairly natural. To base upon them a division of the Romance languages into separate Eastern and Western groups appears unwarranted.

The Romanic Review, **XXXIV** (1943)

IX

AN IMMORTAL CHARACTER IN FRENCH LITERATURE

Recently a friend of mine in the teaching profession remarked: "Spain possesses one of literature's immortal characters, Quijote; Germany has Faușt; England has Hamlet; Italy and France, despite their literary output, have no character that can properly be described as international and deathless."

This is hardly the type of discussion that may be called profitable, though more of it goes on in professional circles than we care to admit. Yet it has its good side, in that it occasionally leads to a note of clarification as to what constitutes literary immortality.

For Italy, it was comparatively easy to reply that Dante, acting in the capacity of his own character, "Man" in the abstract confronting the Deity, had achieved deathlessness.

What of France? My interlocutor smiled politely enough as he mentioned in turn Athalie, Tartuffe, Candide, Jean Valjean, Mme Bovary. I shook my head and proposed Roland. "That's going back pretty far, isn't it?" he asked, "Besides, in what way can Roland be said to be either immortal or representative of mankind?"

The first query, being historical in nature, is easier to answer. If by literary immortality we mean influence, direct of indirect, upon later writers, and acceptance by masses of readers and listeners, these are the facts, in simplified form:

The *Chanson de Roland* influenced all subsequent *Chansons de Geste*, particularly in the *Matière de France*; this is too well known to be dwelt upon. Each of Roland's twelve Peers has his own epic, often accompanied by an *Enfances*. The *Chanson de Geste*, stemming from the Rolan legend, dominates the French twelfth and thirteenth centuries, to be only gradually and in part supplanted by the Breton love-epic.

In the twelfth and early thirteenth centuries particularly, the story of Roland overwhelmingly pervades the scene of world literature, sweeping far beyond national borders to all the countries of western Europe. Provençal, Dutch, German, Norse, Spanish and Welsh versions appear.[1] Of special interest among these are the Swabian *Ruolanteslied,* the Norse-Danish *Karlamagnus Saga* in its Eighth Branch, and the Spanish Pamplona text, of which only a hundred lines survive, enough to indicate fairly close adherence to the French original, at striking variance with the later versions of the Roland legend appearing in the sixteenth-century ballads of Bernardo del Carpio, where the Visigothic barons are the allies of Marsile, and Charlemagne and Roland are depicted in the role of unwelcome invaders. To the twelfth century also belong the French rhymed modernization *Roncevaux,* intended to replace the earlier assonanced version, and the Latin chronicle called the *Pseudo-Turpin,* in which the fighting bishop of Roncevaux, miraculously saved from the slaughter, is supposed to recount his experiences.

Italy apparently received the poem in the thirteenth century, if the Venice Manuscripts are a criterion. What vogue the story of Roland had there may be gauged from the fact that it gave rise to one of the earliest cases on record of a deliberately constructed international language, the Franco-Italian or Franco-Venetian whose ostensible purpose was to permit a French *jongleur* to recount his story to an Italian audience in a tongue close enough to his own to permit the full retention of the original rhythm and assonance, yet near enough to that of his audience to allow them to grasp practically all of his utterances. That the Roland legend had enormous vogue in thirteenth-century Italy is attested by Dante's description of Charlemagne and Roland in Canto XVIII of *Paradise,* as well as by the statues of Roland and Oliver appearing over the doorway of the cathedral of Verona. This architectural detail reminds us that

---

[1] See E. Stengel, *Das altfrz. Rolandslied,* 1900, Introduction; E. Seelmann, *Bibliographie des altfrz. Rolandsliedes,* 1888; L. Gautier, *Bibliographie des Chansons de Geste,* 1897; L. Gautier, *Les Epopées françaises,* II², 279-397; M. Roques in *Romania,* XLVIII (1922), 311 ff; R. Menéndez-Pidal in *Revista de filología española,* IV (1917), 105 ff.

similar artistic tribute was paid to the great literary heroes of the Middle Ages in France (the stained-glass windows of St. Denis and Chartres) and Germany (the *Rolandssäule* of Bremen, first mentioned in 1111). [2]

The Italian late fourteenth, fifteenth and early sixteenth centuries are dominated by the Roland legend. The Franco-Italian *Entrée d'Espagne, Berta e Milone,* the *Orlandino franco-veneto,* Barberino's *Reali di Francia,* Pulci's *Morgante Maggiore,* Boiardo's *Orlando Innamorato,* are only the major works in the Italian cycle that achieves its culmination in Ariosto's *Orlando Furioso,* of which Berni's *Orlando* is a dying echo. [3] And shall we not claim at least an indirect influence upon Tasso's *Gerusalemme Liberata*?

That England knew the legend near its inception and was influenced by it in later centuries is shown by Wace's *Roman de Rou* (III, 8958-62) and by the fifteenth-century *Rowlandes Song* and Caxton's *Life of Charles the Great.* France returns to the theme again and again in Chrétien de Troyes' *Yvain* (3233-7), in the doubtful Latin *Carmine de Proditione Guenonis,* in Aubert's fifteenth-century prose *Conquêtes de Charlemagne.* Holland, after its original thirteenth-century version, returns to the legend in the fifteenth century. Spain is influenced throughout its epic cycle, in the story of the Cid, [4] in Fernán González, in the ballads of Bernardo del Carpio; is it too much to claim that among the "novelas de hazañas y de caballería" which inspired Cervantes in his immortal work, the legend of Roland played an invisible role quite as important, in its own way, as that of Amadís de Gaula?

Roland's legend does not die by the end of the sixteenth century, as some critics seem to think. It lives on, in the minds and hearts of the people, even though spurned by the over-refinement of Europe's seventeenth and eighteenth-century intellectuals.

Doubt was cast, at a time when literary quarrels raged, upon the antiquity of the *Altabiskarco Cantuá,* the brief epic poem described as the Basque reply to the French Song of Roland. But even if its antiquity is in question, its popularity among the Basques is not.

---

[2] See also E. Mâle, *Revue de Paris,* XXVI (1919), 717 ff.
[3] See P. Rajna, *Le Fonti dell'Orlando Furioso,* 1900.
[4] See R. Menéndez-Pidal, *Poema de Mío Cid,* 1913, 38-48.

To this very day, to the writer's personal knowledge, the story of Roland and his heroic deeds, of Charlemagne and Oliver and the twelve Peers lives on in the memory of the lower classes of Italy. The puppet shows so dear to the Italian masses would indeed be incomplete without those great "paladins of France" striking stout blows with tiny wooden swords at the Saracens and the *"perfidi Maganzesi"* who are all that survives of the treacherous line of Ganelon. The literary critics, steeped in a civilization that stems too much from the intellect and too little from the emotions, have forgotten; but the people remember.

* * *

Such are the ramifications of the legendary, literary Roland through the ages, in France and abroad. Surely no character in the world's literature has captivated the collective fancy of mankind to the same degree, penetrating that fancy, directly or indirectly, in straight, diluted or distorted form, through so many lands and ages, and through all classes of society. Other characters live, indeed, in the consciousness, even in the veneration of lovers of literature. But they draw comparatively few imitators or continuators. Who, with the possible exception of Milton, has dared to continue Dante's story of the created face to face with the Creator? Quijote's impractical, desperate idealism has fired the human mind, even to the extent of giving rise to a common adjective, "quixotic"; but what first-class writer has ventured to retell the story of the Gloomy Knight? Above all, who cares to view in Quijote a reflection of himself? Whether we laugh at him or admire him, we shrink from him. And we shrink in like manner from bewildered Hamlet and tortured Faust, despite our absorbed interest in their psychological vicissitudes.

Roland, on the other hand, has popular appeal. His tale is exhumed, resumed, retold by almost countless narrators, some, like Ariosto, definitely in the foremost ranks of literature.

Is this widespread popularity, at all times, in so many places, and in such widely separated social *milieux*, to be scored in Roland's favor or against him? The question is legitimate, for it could plausibly be argued that the very force of popular appeal tends to cheapen a character and distort him beyond all recognition. The

Roland of the Oxford Manuscript and the Orlando of Ariosto have little enough in common. Yet the name of Roland lives on.

Can this be due to the fact that the original Roland, however distorted by successive revampings, is, in the words of my interlocutor, "representative of mankind"? Is he the sort of personage in whom every man can see a reflection of himself—not, perhaps, as he is, but as he would like to be?

I believe the question can be affirmatively answered. The Roland of the original version, whatever be his faults, possesses the positive qualities that appeal to every red-blooded man and woman. He is superlatively the hero; not the hero of illusion, like Quijote; not the hero of doubt and indecision, like Hamlet; not the hero of tormented frustration and vain striving, like Faust; but the hero of strong, decisive, realistic action, the hero that is beloved by both the male and the female of the species. That is the reason why his fame and fortune swept like wildfire over twelfth-century Europe; that is the reason why, even after Turoldus' original tale was lost, the memory and tradition of Roland lived on among the multitudes, in his own and other lands. Other medieval characters grow pale and disappear; Roland's singleness of purpose, his reckless bravery, his unflinching loyalty in the face of overwhelming odds do not permit his memory to fade. He lives on, because he is a symbol: the symbol of courage, determination and sincerity, of faith and trust and piety, of true comradeship and utter sacrifice to a principle and a cause.

It would be inaccurate to say, as some critics may, that Roland captures the fancy of the masses simply because he is symbolical of the strife and bloodshed in which these same masses revel, at least vicariously. Other characters of literature strike mighty blows and slay Saracens by the hundred. Roland's purely military exploits, incredible as they are, pale into insignificance by comparison with those of other characters, in the *Chansons de Geste* and elsewhere.

No, it is the deeper, nobler, more recondite characteristics of the Roland of Turoldus that cause him to stand out in the eyes of the masses, characteristics which less skilled imitators and continuators fail utterly to instil into their creations.

Roland is not merely a warrior. He is a man, endowed with such deeply human qualities that he relives in each and every brave boy sacrificing the flower of his youth upon the altar of a great cause.

Critics say he delights in laying waste towns and countrysides, that his passion is conquest, his idea of amusement to present Charlemagne with all the crowns in the world, typified by a bright red apple. They forget that this is the description of Roland given by his mortal enemy Ganelon; true, perhaps, but deliberately incomplete. Roland is hot-headed indeed, blinded by pride in his own prowess; but not so blind that he does not clearly see through the treachery of Marsile's peace offer and Ganelon's counsel of appeasement. There is a Churchillian or De Gaullish touch about his warning to Charlemagne and the French council: "It would be an evil hour indeed if you trusted Marsile! ...Prosecute the war that you have begun! Lead your hosts to Zaragoza! Lay siege to it with all the means in your power! And avenge those that the traitor put to death!" The entire tragedy of Roncevaux stems from Marsile's false peace offer and the willingness of the Franks to compromise with evil. Roland is impetuous in speech, but clear-headed to the point of prophecy; had his original counsel been followed there would have been no betrayal, no ambush, no loss to the Franks. These details are lost sight of by those who see in Roland only the stubborn pride that leads him to refuse Charlemagne's offer of larger forces and Oliver's frantic plea that he call for reinforcements.

With reference to the latter, how everlastingly human are the reasons for Roland's refusal! He does not want ridicule or the charge of cowardice to attach to himself or his relatives; but above all, it is a sense of national honor and pride that impels him. "May it not please God, or his saints or his angels, that France lose her prestige on my account!" The spirit of the men of Midway, Tobruk and Stalingrad, and all those scattered, outnumbered garrisons, of whatever nationality, that fought to the last rather than take the easy way out.

"Give me liberty or give me death!" said one of our own great men. "Rather would I die than to have disgrace sully my name!" says Roland. And the loyalty of "I regret that I have but one life to give for my country!" is paralleled by Roland's "For one's liege lord must one suffer great pangs, endure great cold and heat, lose his blood and his flesh;" Ask the men of Alamein and Leyte and Sevastopol whether these sentiments are dead.

Roland is harsh to his foes, even after they have fallen; for warfare, in the words of one of our own generals, is a choice between killing and being killed. But he is gentle, even soft, to his own fallen men: "Lords barons, may God have mercy upon you! May He grant paradise to your souls, and let them lie amid holy flowers! I never saw better vassals than you; you served under me so long and so well! French barons, I see you die for me, and I can do nothing to defend or protect you! May the God who never lied help you!" *Mutatis mutandis,* these words might have been spoken by Wainwright of Corregidor, Leopold of the Belgians, or the Duke of Aosta, leaders who chose to share the hopeless fate of their doomed men.

Roland's gentle words to Oliver when the latter strikes him by mistake, his ready forgiveness, his anguish over Oliver's death ("Now that you are dead, it is sad that I must live on!"), his final attempt, when death is already upon him, to bring the bodies of his slain comrades to Turpin so that the latter may bless them, are exquisite touches of that human feeling among true comrades which is deathless through the ages. Seriously wounded American soldiers have been known to offer their blood for buddies whose life depended on an immediate transfusion.

Human indeed is his regret at having to abandon his sword which he has tried in vain to break: "My Durendal! How lovely and white you are! How you reflect the rays of the sun!... For this sword I have grief and sorrow. Rather would I die than let it fall into pagan hands! God the Father, do not permit *that* disgrace to fall upon France!" American artillerymen who could not save or destroy their guns in the great German push on Stavelot died under the Tiger tanks rather than to desert their pieces.

Forever immortal is the profoundly religious spirit in which Roland gives up his soul to his God, along with the right-hand glove that represents the act of feudal homage. Many things pass through his mind in that final moment—his exploits, his beloved country that he will never see again, his relatives, his liege lord. Only Aude is forgotten (or perhaps reverently omitted?), the maiden whose loyalty equals Roland's own, and who later, when she hears Roland is no more, goes to her death uttering words that seem a strange echo of Roland's: "May it not please God or His saints or His angels that after Roland's death I live on!"

Roland contritely begs forgiveness for his sins, both great and small. Facing his Maker, he is as humble as he was fierce and proud when facing his enemies. "Forgive me, Lord, through Thy virtues, for all my sins, from the hour I was born till now, when I lie here! Save my soul from all the perils arising from the sins I committed during my life!" Ask the Army Chaplains whether that deeply reverent spirit does not yet pervade men of all faiths.

Some critics claim that after Roland's death the *Chanson* becomes something of an inferior nature, with characters that move about like gigantic puppets, unendowed with real life. We need not agree with this view, but we can see how it arises. Roland is the great, living character, the one character we get to know, understand, admire and sympathize with to the full, the one completely human character, representing all men, not as they all are, but as they have all, at one time or another in their lives, wanted to be—courageous, chivalrous, devoted, loyal, open-handed and open-hearted, straightforward, honest and sincere, uncompromising with evil, unflinching and unafraid in the service of a lofty principle. A dream of boyhood and early youth, perhaps, from which the crass materialism of later life, the need for "diplomacy", "tact", hypocrisy and double-dealing is the rude awakening; or perhaps, in the case of the men who give up their lives for a cause, a dream from which there is no awakening.

At any rate, Roland endures, because the qualities he represents are undying, and rise up again like a new beacon to summon the youth of each new generation to noble deeds. It remained for recent centuries, epochs of "enlightened" materialism and super-intellective tendencies, to decry those strongly emotional, strongly human qualities and forget Roland and the things he stands for in a vain search for more subtle values that somehow never seem to satisfy. The French in particular, being rather poor salesmen of their own best and most indigenous wares, have failed to portray their own immortal character as he deserves to be portrayed.

But Roland lives on, and will always live. He is the finest and most typical product of that medieval French civilization which bore for its motto: "FAIS CE QUE DOIS, ADVIENNE QUE POURRA."

The French Review, XVIII (1945)

X

ETRUSCAN AND INDO-EUROPEAN CASE-ENDINGS

In a review[1] of Goldmann's *Beiträge zur Lehre vom indogermanischen Charakter der etruskischen Sprache*[2] and of Pallottino's *Elementi di lingua etrusca,*[3] B. A. Terracini states, in refutation of the thesis of the former writer, that while individual lexical elements in Etruscan may well have been borrowed from IE, the more the grammatical structure of Etruscan becomes known to us, the more it reveals itself to be distinct from IE; in support of which, Pallottino's statement[4] is adduced to the effect that Etruscan is, in its phonetic, morphological and lexical foundation, a Mediterranean tongue, more or less closely related to Lemnian, the languages of Asia Minor and perhaps of the pre-Hellenic groups and the pre-IE substratum of Italy.

Pallottino's classification, which appears to be at least partly based upon the findings of Trombetti,[5] derives support from Etruscan morphology, which is "characterized by a lack of definite distinction among individual elements and categories and by the

---

[1] *Archivio Glottologico Italiano,* 1937, 29.1.80.
[2] Heidelberg, 1929-1930.
[3] Firenze, 1936.
[4] *Op. cit.,* 15.
[5] *La lingua etrusca,* Firenze, 1928. It may be stated at this point that no responsibility is assumed by the present writer for the Etruscan case-endings presented by Trombetti and Pallottino and, in the case of the latter writer, accepted, at least by implication, by favorable reviewers (cf. Terracini, *AGI* 29.1.80; R. P. Kent, *Language,* 13.4.331-332, etc.). The only purpose of this article is to point out the correspondences between these hypothetical endings and those of IE.

phenomenon of grammatical redetermination appearing side by side with a flexional system, which leads to an abundance of morphological variants and great complexity and freedom for Etruscan grammatical formations, governed by laws which are altogether unexplainable by analogy with the IE tongues".

While this singular complexity and freedom appears undeniable, it would also appear that too little importance has been granted by the two Italian Etruscologists to the fundamental flexional system which they themselves postulate.

A comparison of the table of singular case-endings and of the one more or less definitely established plural ending presented by Trombetti [6] with the corresponding endings of the IE declensional scheme [7] results in the accompanying table of correspondences:

	ā-stems		i-stems		o-stems		u-stems		consonant-stems		ē-stems	
	IE	ETR	IE	ETR	IE	ETR	IE	ETR	IE	ETR	IE	ETR
NOM. SG.	ā	a(s)	is	I(s)	os	us	u(s)		s, O	s, O	ēs	e(s)
GEN. SG.	ās	as	eis, ois	iś, eis	osyo, oso	eus, ous	us, auś	es, os, s	ś	ēs, ēI (anal.?)	es
DAT. SG.	āi	e	eyei	ei	ōi	ewei, ewai	ui	ei, ai	e	ēi, ei (anal.?)	?
ACC. SG.	ām	a	im	i	om	um	u	m, O	O	em, ēm	e
LOC. SG.	āi	ati	eyi, ē(i)	iti	oi, ei	ewi, ēu	uø	i, O	ōi	?	eōi
INSTR. SG.	abhi		ibhi		obhi	ubhi		bhi		?		
ABL. SG.					ōd, ēd or ōt, ēt						ēd (?)	
"GEN-DAT. PL."		aśi		iśi				uśi		śi		eśi
LOC. PL.	āsu		isu		oisu		usu		su		?	

---

[6] *Op. cit.*, 22.

[7] Brugmann, *Grundriss der vergleichenden Grammatik der indogermanischen Sprachen*, Strassburg, 1897-1916, 2.122 ff.

Pallottino [8] accepts Trombetti's table practically in its entirety. The only important deviations from Trombetti's scheme are the following: 1) for the dat.-loc. of $\bar{a}$-stems, Pallottino establishes a form in *-ai* for older Etruscan, corresponding to *-e* for the more recent inscriptions; this brings the Etruscan form even more definitely in line with the IE; 2) a dat.-loc. *-ei* is offered for *e*-stems, which again approaches the IE *-ēi, -ei*; 3) the *-śi* form, which Trombetti advances as a plural on the basis of plural use in *clenar-a-śi, precu θur-a-si*,[9] is by Pallottino treated as an emphatic extension of the *s*-genitive.

The general resemblance of the two sets of flexional endings is striking, and we must attribute the fact that it was overlooked by both Trombetti and Pallottino to the preoccupation of the former to connect Etruscan with the Lemnian and Caucasian groups as well as with IE, thus bringing it in line with his general theories on linguistic monogenesis, and to the emphasis placed by the latter upon what appear to be secondary formations.

If we examine the correspondences in detail, we note the following facts:

1. Etruscan appears to possess a full declension of *e*-stems, which is rare in IE.[10] IE, on the other hand, possesses a full declension of *o*-stems, which in Etruscan seem to have merged with the *u*-stems. Note, however, that IE *o*-stems are more properly *e/o*-stems, the *e*-grade appearing in the vocative singular and in alternative forms of several other cases. This *e*-grade appears to have become generalized in Etruscan, as Trombetti suggests.[11]

2. In the nominative singular, Etruscan occasionally makes use of the *s*-suffix, but more often uses the simple theme.[12] It may be that this indecision in the use of final *-s* in Etruscan may be connected with the similar phenomenon of Italic.[13]

3. Little is to be said concerning the genitive endings,[14] which,

---

[8] *Op. cit.*, 40.
[9] *Op. cit.*, 17.
[10] Lat. *diēs, rēs*; Gk. χρή; Skt. *çraddhā-*; Lith. (*-iē*) *žemė*; Buck, *Comparative Grammar of Greek and Latin*, § 273.
[11] *Op. cit.*, 13.
[12] Trombetti, 13-14; Pallottino, 38.
[13] Buck, § 212.2; Grandgent, *Introduction to Vulgar Latin*, § 298.
[14] Trombetti, 16-18; Pallottino, 38.

in the case of *ā*-stems, were definitely claimed by an earlier Etruscologist [15] as pure Etruscan, not borrowed from Italic, but corresponding to Italic-Latin -*ās*, Greek -ᾱ·ς, -ης, Vedic -*ās* and Gothic -*ōs*.

4. Little is also to be said concerning the Etruscan dative-locative endings, [16] which, especially in Pallottino's classification, appear to correspond very closely to the IE dative endings.

5. With regard to the accusative endings of Etruscan, attention may be drawn to Trombetti's statement [17] that such endings, particularly in the older language, often appear with an -*n* (occasionally -*m*) suffix. Pallottino [18] denies that there is any definite trace of a distinction between the nominative and the accusative. If Trombetti's view is accepted, attention must again be called, as in the case of the -*s* suffix for the nominative, to the similar state of affairs in Italic. [19]

6. In the case of Trombetti's locative in -*ti*, -*θi*, -*θ*, [20] there appears to be no direct correspondence with IE locative endings. Trombetti compares these endings with Greek adverbial πό-θι, οικο-θι, ἀγρό-θι. αὖ-τι, προ-τί, Sk. *pra-ti*, Hittite *e-ti*, agreeing in this with Deecke. [21] Two other possibilities, however, present themselves.

Bugge [22] advances the theory, supported by abundant examples, that Etruscan *θ* corresponds to Italic *f*. If this contention is accepted, the phonetic development might be assumed to be the following: IE *bh* > Italic *f* > Etruscan *θ* (represented in Etruscan inscriptions indifferently by *θ* or *t*). In this case, we should have a complete series of correspondences between the Etruscan locative and the IE instrumental endings (-*abhi*: -*ati*: *ibhi*: -*iti*; -*ubhi*: -*uθ*; -*bhi*: -*θi*).

On the other hand, the ablative singular ending of IE *o*-stems (-*ōd*, -*ēd*, or -*ōt*, -*ēt*) offers an excellent correspondence for Etruscan

---

[15] W. Deecke, *Etruskische Forschungen und Studien*, 5.114, 1883.
[16] Trombetti, 14-15; Pallottino, 39.
[17] Trombetti, 14.
[18] Pallottino, 39.
[19] Buck, § 212.1.
[20] Trombetti, 15-16; Pallottino, 39.
[21] *Etr. Forsch. u. Stud.*, 2.62, 1882.
[22] *Beiträge zur Erforschung der etruskischen Sprache*, Stuttgart, 1883, 201-203.

-$u\theta$, which, interestingly enough, is offered without a final vowel for the *u*-stem declension. The extension of the IE ablative *o*-stem ending to cover all Etruscan so-called locative singular endings could then be postulated, with, perhaps, a crossing of this ending with the vocalic termination of IE locative or instrumental endings to account for the vocalic termination of Etruscan *-ati*, *-iti*, and *-θi*.

7. The only series of endings for which Trombetti advances a definite plural possibility is the so-called genitive-dative *-aśi*, *-isi*, *-usi*, *-śi*, *-eśi*. The locative plural endings of IE, which most closely correspond to this series, have *-u* as a final vowel. It is to be noted, however, that Greek has a dative plural in *-σι*, which is explained as representing an alternative form to *-su* in the IE parent language, or a special modification due to the influence of *-i* in the dative-locative singular. [23] It is true that the Etruscan endings in question are not universally looked upon as plural, but considered by some as alternative to the more common *e/i* terminations accepted for the dative singular. This interpretation, however, is not definitely established, while the form *clenaraśi* seems to point quite definitely to a plural use.

It is quite true that this discussion leaves out of account several additional case-forms which have been postulated for Etruscan (the "genitival" formations in *-l*, *-a*, *-al*, *-ia*; "genitival" combinations of *-s* and *-l*; [24] dative forms in *-ri*; [25] the secondary feminine declensional system postulated by Pallottino [26]). But these forms, in addition to being less definite and certain than the others, also appear to fall in with Pallottino's classification of "grammatical redetermination, consisting essentially in the superposing of suffixes, akin or varied in nature, in order better to determine the syntactical function of a given form", which appears to exist in Etruscan "side by side with flexion". [27]

---

[23] Buck, § 230.10.
[24] Trombetti, 18-20; Pallottino, 38. The comparatively late appearance of these combinations is, however, claimed by Danielsson, *CIE* 5093, 1.61, and *Le monde oriental*, 1908, 2.240; Herbig, *IF*, 26.369 n.; and Hempl, *Mediterranean Studies*, 4.22.
[25] Trombetti, 21; Pallottino, 39.
[26] Pallottino, 41-42.
[27] Pallottino, 15.

Concerning the nature and origin of this phenomenon of redetermination, which appears unconnected with IE, we are in no position to pronounce. On the other hand, the flexional system proper, as postulated by Trombetti and Pallottino, appears to be definitely connected with IE, and brings back to mind the statement made, in connection with a study of Etruscan proper names by Deecke: [28] "Ich betone dabei wieder, dass ich die Beimischung eines starken fremdartigen Elements durchaus anerkenne, aber ich halte, trotz der theilweise wundersamen Umgestaltung des vorgefundenen geformten Sprachmaterials und der unläugbaren argen Zersetzung des sprachlichen Organismus, dennoch das indogermanisch-italische Element im Etruskischen für überwiegend und für die eigentliche Grundlage des Ganzen."

Italica, XXII (1945)

---

[28] *Op. cit.,* 5.148.

XI

REFLECTIONS ON THE ORIGIN OF THE ROMANCE LANGUAGES

Julien Bonfante is to be thanked for having brought forward again, in these days of current emphasis on intensely practical language studies, the important historical question of the origin of the Romance languages. [1]

Are these languages, he asks, a product of the decomposition of Imperial and Christian Latin, or did they begin to arise at the time of the various Roman colonizations? It is essential that this question be answered, he points out, because a 1000-year linguistic period is involved. If the former hypothesis is valid, a fairly unified Latin was spoken over the entire Latin domain from the Punic Wars to the time of Charlemagne; if the latter, proto-Romance tongues were in existence from the end of the first Punic War, increasing in number and variety with each new advance of the Roman legions. The fact that today, in spite of easy communications and widespread education, there is an infinite variety of French, Italian, German and Slavic dialects, says Bonfante, is indirect evidence that an even greater variety must have existed at a time when communications were primitive and illiteracy widespread.

The autor might have added English to his list of highly dialectalized tongues; the English of Britain, not the English of the United States, a country which in many respects resembles the ancient Roman Empire. [2]

---

[1] *Renaissance*, I, 4 (1943), 573-588.
[2] See my *Italian Language* (New York, 1941), p. 15, for this comparison.

For the commercial, political, and, consequently, linguistic importance of what Bonfante calls "primitive means of communication" he may be referred to a historian of the Latin language, G. Devoto [3] while for his allusion to "l'instruction publique à peu près nulle, l'analphabétisme régnant" the ancient writers cited by Mohl [4] and Budinszky [5] are enlightening. The fact that there were popular, plebean schools in Rome and Italy from the days of the Etruscan kings to the end of the Republic, [6] and in all the provinces under the Empire [7] and even after the fall of the Empire, [8] and the existence of the government-endowed *grammatici* instituted in the later days of the Empire in all towns and hamlets, [9] are of considerable interest, particularly when we recall that our own system of modern education is less than a century old, and that widespread illiteracy was the norm in the countries of Europe down to the Napoleonic Wars and beyond.

R. A. Hall, Jr., reviewing this work in *Language*, XIX, 3 (1941), 267, erroneously states that I claim "an absolute Pre-Romance unity (which is wrongly compared to a supposed absolute unity of American English) lasting all through the time of the Empire and much later". This is what I actually say: "the linguistic conditions prevailing in the western portion of the Empire at the time of its greatest extent resembled not so much those of modern European countries as those of present-day United States—general linguistic standardization, a few local peculiarities in the unassimilated backwoods corresponding to our immigrant dialects, a few local differences of intonation and vocabulary corresponding to our southern, New England, and western traits, and a widespread tendency toward slang and raciness of language; rather than clear-cut 'Gaulish', 'Iberian', 'Oscan' or 'African' Latin, or a universal spoken 'Vulgar Latin' in direct contrast with an artificial, literary 'classical Latin' used solely by the writers". Mutual comprehensibility and general standardization are not synonymous with "absolute linguistic unity".

[3] G. Devoto, *Storia della lingua di Roma*, Bologna, 1940; see also Cicero, *Pro Fonteio*, V, II, for the interchange of goods, money and people that took place by means of the Roman roads.

[4] G. Mohl, *Introduction à la chronologie du latin vulgaire*, Paris, 1899.

[5] A. Budinszky, *Die Verbreitung der lateinischen Sprache*, Berlin, 1881, pp. 104-108.

[6] Livy, III, 44; IX, 36; Pliny the Younger, *Epist.*, IV, 13; Seneca, *Ep.*, 88; Plautus, *Mercat.*, II, 2, 32; Horace, *Ep.*, I, XX, 17; Quintilian, I, XXVII, 1; I, II, 4; Macrobius, *Saturn.*, I, 12; Suetonius, *Caesar*, 42.

[7] Plutarch, *Sertor.*, 14; Livy, XLIII, 3; Tacitus, *Ann.*, III, 43; Eumenius, *Oratio pro instaur. schol.*, 3; Suetonius, *De illustr. gramm.*, 3; Tacitus, *Agricola*, XXI.

[8] Grober, *Archiv für lat. Lex.*, I, 49.

[9] *Theodosian Code*, XIII, tit. III, 11.

An interesting comparison is established by the author. The Latin language, he tells us, resembles a river along whose course several canals are cut. The river's water, pure near the source, picks up various impurities as it goes along. Each of the intersecting canals will receive water contaminated by the impurities previously absorbed. By the time the stream reaches the sea it will have acquired its maximum of impurities. This stream, in Bonfante's concept, is the Latin language. The countries of earliest colonization are the first intersecting canals; their language is purer, closer to the original Latin; later colonizations carry more impurities, *i.e.*, more numerous and glaring linguistic changes. The stream that finally reaches the sea, charged with assorted impurities, is Italian, the direct continuator of Latin. This means that Italian should diverge from Classical Latin to a greater degree than any of the other Romance languages. Does Mr. Bonfante seriously hold that Italian diverges from Latin more than Spanish or French? [10]

This "chronological" theory of Romance development is, of course, far from new. As Bonfante points out, it was first advanced by Gröber in 1884. [11] It was, as he says, "presque totalement oubliée ensuite", and for very good reasons. If there is anything that serious chronological studies of the Latin language show us, it is that while Latin was indeed changing during the entire period of Roman expansion (as all living languages change), the *rate* of change was relatively slow, and the features of change absolutely insufficient to account for later Romance differentiation. [12] On the other hand, the fact that change appears throughout definitely acquits the Latin of Classical literature, that of the inscriptions and of the post-Classical texts, of the charge that it is a static, crystallized tongue like the high Wên-li of China or the Classical Arabic of the Koran. A tongue that

---

[10] I assume that by "Italian" he means the central variety, more or less coinciding with the literary tongue, rather than the Gallo-Italian or Venetian varieties of the North or the Neapolitan-Abruzzese or Calabrian-Sicilian of the South. It is this central, more or less literary Italian which is, geographically and historically, the most direct continuator of Latin.

[11] *Archiv für lat. Lex.*, I (1884), 210 ff.

[12] See Devoto. *op. cit.*; R. G. Kent, *The Sounds of Latin*, Baltimore, 1932.

changes as Latin changed in the pre-Classical, Classical and post-Classical periods is definitely a living, spoken tongue.

The phenomena involved in earlier changes of the Latin language are largely irrelevant from the standpoint of later Romance dialectalization. Inscriptional material and all other evidence at our disposal are equally inconclusive from the standpoint of dialectalization during the Classical period.[13] The consciousness of a linguistic difference between *lingua latina* and *lingua romana rustica* does not appear till the time of Charlemagne.

Bonfante establishes, through the treatment of accented Latin vowels in their various Romance developments and in borrowings by Germanic and Celtic tongues, a threefold chronological series: first, a "Sardinian" stage, reflecting the vocalism of the third century B.C.; second, a "Roumanian" stage, reflecting the vocalism of the first century A.D.; third, a "French-Spanish-Italian" stage, reflecting the vocalism of the fourth century A.D. There is nothing to prevent our acceptance of this principle. But the author should be reminded: first, that it works definitely against the "chronological" theory, since by his own admission [14] it would indicate that Iberia and Gaul developed not in accordance with the chronology of conquest, but in accord with innovations coming from Italy; second, that the French-Spanish-Italian stage is reached quite late (no earlier than the fourth century A.D.) if his copious examples of borrowings by the Germanic and Celtic tongues are to be taken into account, for these borrowings reflect, "between the second and the fourth centuries A.D.", a vocalic system in which $\breve{\imath}$ and $\bar{e}$, $\breve{u}$ and $\bar{o}$, and even $\breve{a}$ and $\bar{a}$ are carefully kept distinct.

The author's discussion of chronology in connection with the fall of final *-s* in Italy and Dacia and its conservation in the western provinces lends itself to other considerations. It is true that final *-s*

---

[13] See Budinszky, *op. cit.*, K. Sittl, *Die lokalen Verschiedenheiten der lateinischen Sprache*, Erlangen, 1882; E. Diehl, *Vulgärlateinische Inschriften*, Bonn, 1910.

[14] P. 582: "Il semble donc que les déformations vocaliques qui caractérisent l'italien, l'espagnol et le français n'avaient pas pénétré en Gaule et en Grande-Bretagne au temps de ces emprunts. Ces transformations sont donc, comme la plupart des transformations romanes, d'origine italienne."

tends to disappear in many inscriptional forms in the third century A.D.; but the identical widespread fall of final -*s* is also characteristic of the inscriptions of the fourth and third centuries B.C. [15] Should not this *early* fall of final -*s* (later checked by the grammarians) have been reflected in Sardinian and Spanish development if the chronological theory is correct? And does Mr. Bonfante really believe that the legionaries and colonists who went to Dacia after 107 A.D., bringing with them a final -*s*-less tongue, [16] all came from Italy? Were there no Gauls, Spaniards or other non-Italians in Trajan's legions? [17]

If there is one thing which stands out clearly from Bonfante's demonstration, it seems to be that the Latin of Spain, Gaul and Italy held remarkably well together down to the fourth century A.D., and that this universal spoken Latin of the major, contiguous Romance areas had not even advanced to the point of merging $\bar{e}$ and $\breve{\imath}$, $\bar{o}$ and $\breve{u}$, or of obliterating Classical quantities.

If the greater conservatism of Sardinia and Dacia with respect to stressed vowels, and such other phenomena as the fall of final -*s* and -*t* are enough to warrant a claim for nascent and separate Romance languages, then we might also be justified in saying that Midwestern [ba:t], [ka:t] for *bought, caught,* Bostonese [ka:nt], [ba:θ], for *can't, bath,* and the Southern fall of final -*r* vs. its retention in "general" American permit us to speak, at the present time of nascent and separate American languages.

The test of linguistic unity is mutual comprehension. It would be idle to deny the existence of minor linguistic variations in a territory as extensive as the Roman Empire. The question is whether these linguistic variations were of the same nature and extent as the present-day American "dialects", or whether they were the

---

[15] Devoto, *op. cit.,* pp. 100-101; Kent, *op. cit.,* p. 57.

[16] The fall of final -*s* appears in numerous inscriptions of western as well as eastern Romania; for a few examples which contradict both Bonfante and Carnoy, whom the former cites to the effect that the inscriptions of Spain show fall of final -*s* only at the end of the line, indicating that it is an orthographic abbreviation, see *Corpus Inscriptionum Latinarum,* II, 5393; XIII, 2000; XII, 923; and particularly II, 5416 and II, 1876.

[17] H. Gooss, *Arch. Vereins siebenb. Landesk.,* XII, 1 (1874), 107-166, gives a list of Trajan's auxiliaries, who were for the most part Spaniards, Rhetians and Syrians. Suetonius, *Vespas.,* 6, states that during the reign of Nero the Legio III Gallica moved to Moesia to fight the Dacians.

profound, irreconcilable differences occurring between Sicilian and Piedmontese, Norman and Provençal, Castilian, Galician and Catalan. All the evidence adduced so far, including that presented by Bonfante, is in favor of the former theory. The big linguistic cleavages that mark the Romance world are apparently of a later date —a date that seems to come close to their actual appearance in recorded form.

As for the causes of this conservatism of the Latin tongue even after the Empire's fall, they have been admirably set forth in detail by H. F. Muller.[18] Chief among them are the immense prestige of the former Empire's tongue among the former Empire's populations and the incoming barbarians,[19] and the fact that Latin, adopted as the language of the western Church and of Christianization while the Empire was at the height of its splendor, continued, in spite of all political and social upheavals during the three centuries that followed the Empire's fall, to be the tongue of both Church and Christianization.[20]

The Romanic Review, XXXVI (1945)

---

[18] "A Chronology of Vulgar Latin", ZRP, Supplement 78, 1929.
[19] Mohl, *op. cit.*, pp. 69-71.
[20] Mohl, *op. cit.*, pp. 166-168.

XII

AB AND THE SURVIVAL OF THE LATIN GENITIVE IN OLD ITALIAN

Antonio Mezzacappa advances the theory [1] that the use of the oblique case Old French and of the single case in Old Italian, without a preposition, to express the genitive relation goes back to a use of *ab*, which is said to have disappeared by reason of absorption when used after first-declension nouns.

I find myself definitely in agreement with Mezzacappa for what concerns the survival of *ab* in Romance. Despite the claims of Grandgent, [2] *ab* does not seem to have disappeared from the Romance languages. It survives to the present day in Provençal and Catalan *ab, amb,* used in the sense of "with". (These forms are claimed to hare come from *apud,* but the evidence for this is doubtful.) In early Old French, *ab* appears likewise with the meaning of "with" (never "from" or "of"). [3] Why should we accept Old French *ab* as coming from *apud* when *apud* appears in Old French as *od*? [4] For what concerns Italian, the survival of *ab* seems attested, though only in the combined form *de ab (daba, da).* [5]

However, the absorption of *a* (< *ab*) in such expressions as *de la camera a suum patrem* > *de la cameraa som padre* > *de la chambre son pedre* seems controverted by the fact that prepositional *a* re-

---

[1] *Italica,* XXIV, 3, 248-250.
[2] *An Introduction to Vulgar Latin,* 10, 39.
[3] *Oaths of Strasbourg: et ab Ludher nul plaid nunquam prindrai;* also *Passion,* 132, 260, 427, 451, 488, 504; *Léger* 8, 228.
[4] *Alexis* strophe 43, 122, *et pass.; Roland, pass.*
[5] Pei, The Italian Language (Columbia, N. Y., 1941), 116.

"AB" AND THE SURVIVAL OF THE LATIN GENITIVE IN OLD ITALIAN 121

mains unchanged in French, while the final -*a* of first-declension nouns turns into mute -*e*. Absorption of the strong prepositional *a* by the weak, unstressed final mute -*e* is unlikely. We should rather expect the opposite to take place, with elision of the final mute -*e* of the noun, and a resultant *chambr'a son pedre*. Lastly, the analogy whereby this disappearance of the preposition *a* would be extended to cases where an original final -*a* did not precede the preposition (*la maison a son pedre* > *la maison son pedre*) seems questionable.

Furthermore, the use of the oblique case (not the accusative!) without a preposition in the genitive function is so abundantly attested in the Vulgar Latin documents of France as to be beyond question, [6] while the use of *ab* to indicate possession is not apparent in Vulgar Latin writings; [7] on the contrary, the use of *ad* to replace *ab* or to denote possession is fairly common. [8]

With respect to the theory that the practice of denoting possession without any preposition in Italian spread from remnants of the Latin genitive, Mezzacappa states that I do not explain how such a construction evolved. At the risk of being repetitious, I may here summarize the evolution I traced in *Lingua Nostra*. [9]

While French preserves final -*s* and first merges, then drops all final vowels save -*a*, Italian drops final -*s* and keeps a considerable measure of distinction in final vowels. Consequently, the French documents of the 8th century show a strong tendency to use a single oblique case in all oblique functions, including the genitive, while the Italian documents of the same period show a rather careful conservation of masculine genitive singular forms in -*i*. This state of affairs is reflected in the two Romance languages themselves when their vernacular documents begin to appear: French uses the oblique without a preposition in the genitive function; Italian shows, down to the 13th century, the conservation of genitive forms in -*i*. For

---

[6] Pei, *The Language of the Eighth-Century Texts in Northern France* (N. Y., 1932), 218-222.

[7] R. W. Scott, *The Prepositions ab, apud and cum* (Tokyo 1937), 48-49, 60, 62; he speaks also of the fact that *a* (*ab*) was reinforced in Vulgar Latin by being constantly used with the final -*b*, and specifically mentions that *a* < *ad* was felt to be quite distinct from *ab*.

[8] Pei, *The Language of the Eighth-Century Texts in Northern France*, 238-241.

[9] *Lingua Nostra*, I, 4, 101-103.

the examples, which are fairly numerous, the reader is referred to the original *Lingua Nostra* article.

The following statistical comparison, which was not available at the time of the *Lingua Nostra* article, is instructive:

The original French eighth-century documents of Tardif's collection have a total of 108 masculine proper names used in the genitive function. The Classical *-i* ending appears in only 19 of these (18 % of all cases); while in 89 cases (82 % of the total) it is replaced by the oblique ending *-o*. [10]

The Italian eighth-century documents appearing in Bonelli's *Codice diplomatico longobardo* have 130 masculine proper names used in the genitive function. Among these, the Classical ending in *-i* appears in 77 cases (59 % of the total); it is replaced by the oblique *-o* ending in 15 instances (11 % of the total); while the remaining 38 cases (30 % of the total) consist of Longobardic names used in the genitive relation without any Latin ending (*Vualterat, Vulfram*, etc.). [11]

This discrepancy in two sets of contemporary documents which in other respects present largely identical phenomena is striking, and seems to point definitely to the later separate trends of the two Romance languages. It may be added that *ab* is never used to express the genitive relation, with proper or with common nouns, in either set of documents.

Italica, V (1948)

---

[10] Pei, *The Language of the Eighth-Century Texts in Northern France*, 377.

[11] These figures are drawn from a Columbia doctoral dissertation by Robert Politzer, entitled *A Study of the Language of the Eighth-Century Lombardic Documents*.

A more comprehensive study of 7th and 8th century documents from northern Italy appearing in *Romance Trends in 7th and 8th Century Latin Documents*, by Frieda N. Politzer and Robert Politzer (University of North Carolina Press, 1953) gives the following figures: out of a total of 1697 genitive forms, 1052 (62 %) show *-i*; 136 (8 %) show *-o*; 476 (28 %) are Germanic names without any Latin ending. The remaining 33 (2 %) are endings in *-u, -us, -e, -os*.

XIII

A NEW METHODOLOGY FOR ROMANCE CLASSIFICATION

In the field of Romance linguistics, we are often struck by statements of two types. The first concerns the relative conservatism or tendency to innovation of individual Romance varieties. A given language or dialect is described as "practically Latin in unchanged state, spoken to the present day" in a given area. The areas most favored for this treatment are, usually, the Rheto-Rumansh and the Rumanian. This type of statement is often characteristic of the nonspecialist, and is equally often induced by nationalistic considerations, but it is occasionally coiced by people who ought to know better. One of my old professors of Romance linguistics, now dead, used to preface his introduction of a Rumanian speaker to the class with the words: "Gentlemen, you are now about to hear what is practically pure, ancient Latin". Similar statements, though modified and disguised, occur in the writings of some of our best-known contemporary linguists, who describe Rumanian, Rheto-Rumansh, Sardinian, Portuguese, etc. as 'archaic' on the ground of one of two conservative features on which they fasten their attention to the exclusion of everything else. In like manner other areas, like the Castilian or northern French, are described as "radiating centers of innovation" by reason of certain phenomena which strike the fancy, but which may be no more indicative of innovation tendencies than dozens of others that are overlooked.

The second type of statement consists of a set of implications based upon real or fancied similarities occurring in two or more Romance varieties which may or may not be contiguous. Recently one of my students endeavored to establish some sort of linguistic, historical and cultural connection between the Gascon and the Franco-Provençal areas on the sole basis of the change of initial *v* to *b*. While this particular outburst was repressed with comparative ease, others, advanced by scholars of standing, have found their way into accredited manuals. Ascoli's claim of a separate Franco-Provençal classification was originally based largely on the single phenomenon of the treatment of stressed *a* when following or not following a palatal or guttural. The defense of Catalan as a Spanish rather than a Provençal variety is still based mainly on the conservation of Latin *ū*. A "fundamental unity" between two or more Romance varieties is postulated on the ground of one or two phenomena which those varieties display in common, as when an "East Romance" consisting of Italian south of an imaginary Spezia-Rimini line, Dalmatian and Rumanian is constructed out of the fall of final *-s*, supported, but not validly, by a supposed non-voicing of intervocalic occlusives. The only wonder is that it has not yet occurred to some ambitious linguist to claim a fundamental unity between Italian and Picard based on similarity of palatalization before the various classes of vowels.

The time has perhaps come to replace this somewhat haphazard methodology of classification with some system of measurements that will take into account not merely one or two individual features, but the sum total of the important features characterizing Romance languages and dialects, for the purpose of defining more clearly the relationships among them, and between any one of them and the Latin from which they issued.

In the past, historical grammar has followed an inductive system, largely based, however, upon the individual language or dialect, isolated from its fellows and placed under the spotlight. The phonology, morphology, syntax and vocabulary of individual tongues have been successively described, as in Bourciez' "Éléments de linguistique romane"; or, as in Meyer-Lübke's "Grammatik der romanischen Sprachen", the various languages have been compared, item by item, but with no attempt to summarize these lengthy series of comparisons or to draw general conclusions from them. Perhaps it was felt that the description of languages or phenomena was all that could be accomplished from the standpoint of strict linguistic science. It was also perhaps overlooked that while a conclusion based on insufficient factual evidence is unscientific, a display of factual evidence without conclusions is, to say the least, unsatisfactory.

In one division of linguistic description, and one only, has some attempt been made to apply a thoroughly scientific, statistical method. This field is vocabulary. The lexicologist who is, in a sense, a statistician of language, is able to tell us precisely what percentage of the words in a language like French consists of Latin roots, what percentage of Greek, Celtic, Germanic roots, or words historically borrowed from other Romance languages, or from English, Semitic, Slavic, etc. He can establish these proportions for the language at any stage. Using works like Godefroy's, he can tell us precisely what the Old French vocabulary of the 11th, 12th or 13th century consisted of. By a word-count of literary documents, he can give us a precise picture of the frequency of occurrence of words of various origins. He is in a position to tell, for instance, that in the literary vocabulary of the 12th century the proportion of Latin words was 75 %, of Greek words 10 %, of Germanic words 13 %; but that if these words are considered with respect to frequency of occurrence, Latin rises to 85 %, Germanic sinks to 9 % and Greek to 5 %. In this fashion, fantasies are repressed, and the language is placed in its proper perspective. An imaginative linguist whose fancy has been struck by the seemingly high number of Germanic loan-words in the "Chanson de Roland", and who is consequently tempted to assign to the Germanic element in the Old French vocabulary too much importance can at once be set right, by the presentation of definite statistics.

This statistical method has unfortunately never been applied to the other divisions of linguistic change: phonology, morphology, syntax. It has possibly been deemed too difficult of application. The values that would have to be assigned to individual change-phenomena are perhaps considered too arbitrary. Yet, unless we take the bull by the horns and attempt the experiment, we shall forever be condemned to listen to such unscientific pronouncements as the ones described above.

What it is proposed to demonstrate is that the comparative statistical method can perhaps be applied on a far more extensive scale than has hitherto been the case. By taking the various general processes of change in the fields of phonology, morphology and syntax, assigning to them some sort of numerical value, and applying this value to the phenomena as they occur in the individual languages and dialects, we may possibly be able to achieve a more precise basis of comparison among the individual languages, or between any one of them and the original Latin.

Let us give a brief and very incomplete demonstration of this tentative methodology, which is all that the space at our diposal permits. For the purposes of this demonstration, we shall restrict ourselves to a single division of phonology, accented vocalism, and to seven of the principal Romance varieties: standard literary French, Spanish, Italian, Portuguese and Rumanian, standard literary Old Provençal, and Logudorese Sardinian. A fuller demonstration, including unstressed vowels, consonants, the divisions of morphology and those of syntax, and applied to a larger number of Romance varieties, is reserved for a lengthier work.

The Classical Latin system of accented vowels consisted of five long and five short vowels, plus three commonly used diphthongs, of which two, *ae* and *oe*, merge universally in development with certain vowels, while only one, *au*, has a separate development. (*Eu*, which has rare and doubtful survival save in learned words, may be omitted from our calculations.) Within four out of the five pairs of long and short vowels, it is generally recognized that a qualitative as well as a quantitative difference existed. Since quantity as such is not a factor in Romance development, it may be disregarded for our purpose. Quality, on the other hand, is highly significant in Romance development. There is only one pair of vowels, long and short *a*, which coincide universally in Romance development. We may therefore consider the significant Latin stressed vowel-sounds as ten, regardless of the fact that some of the fell together in some Romance languages. The two *a*'s fall together in all Romance languages, but by reason of frequency of occurrence as a long and as a short Latin vowel, *a*, for statistical purposes, is counted twice to the other vowels' once.

These stressed vowel-sounds show a mass of changes in the various Romance languages, depending on their position (free, checked, before nasals, before or after palatals, before umlaut-producing final vowels, etc.). If we assign a more or less arbitrary numerical value to the various possibilities of change, we shall reach a total which will represent the maximum possible Romance deviation from the original Latin. Obviously, no one language or dialect will attain this maximum. Each language, however, will score a certain number of points in connection with the possible changes. This score, reduced to percentages, will give us the coefficient of innovation for any given variety, for what concerns accented vocalism.

Two points may here be stressed: 1. We do no include in our count phenomena of irregular, occasional, or arbitrary occurrence, such as vocalic assimilation or dissimilation, or changes of an analogical nature; only such phenomena as tend to assume a regular pattern in at least one of the languages under consideration are included; 2. The point values assigned are, for the time being, frankly arbitrary; as the system is applied, it will probably be found desirable to make numerous changes in point distribution, and to add other phenomena which may at first have been overlooked.

On the basis of our point distribution, we have a maximum of 77 change-points assigned to stressed vowel-sounds. With *a* counted twice, there are 11 such sounds, and they may occur in the free or in the checked position. The maximum number of change-points assigned to any one vowel in one position (free or checked) is 3½. The maximum amount of change that may occur in a stressed vowel is generally conceded to be diphthongization, for which 2 points are assigned. Lesser change consists of a modification in the quality of the vowel, for which 1 point is assigned. Conditioned phenomena of change, such as nasalization or other change due to the influence of a following nasal; changes due to the influx of a preceding or following palatal (such as Castilian $a > e$ in forms like *lactem* > *leche*); umlaut phenomena, which in languages like Rumanian and Portuguese occur with regularity, and in others, like French and Castilian, sporadically, but with some frequency ($illī > il$, $vigintī > vingt$, $fecī > hice$), are rated at ½ point. The failure to effect a normal change by reason of a following palatal, nasal or liquid (as in Castilian *noche, espejo,* Italian *consiglio, pugno*), or by reason of hiatus position (Italian *via, tuo*) is considered as a negative phenomenon from the standpoint of change, and is rated at minus ½ point. Failure to effect any change whatsoever in the quality of the vowel gives 0 points.

The detailed application of this point system to the stressed vowel development in each of the languages under consideration appears in the accompanying charts. The final result turned from points into percentages of change, permits us to state that on the basis of our tentative point-system the percentage of stressed-vowel change from the original Latin for each of the seven languages is as follows: French, 44%; Portuguese, 31%; Provençal, 25%; Rumanian, 23½%; Spanish, 20%; Italian, 12%; Sardinian, 8%.

This very elementary, incomplete and tentative demonstration shows us which languages have departed furthest from the original Latin with respect to accented vocalism, and also the extent to which they have diverged. It shows us which languages may rightly be called more conservative or more innovating in this particular respect. It permits us to place any individual dialect in the scale and assign it to a rightful place. It also permits an immediate comparison to be made between any two languages or dialects, for purposes of classification and affiliation.

When to the score for accented vowels we shall be in a position to add the various scores for unaccented vowels in the various positions, we shall have achieved a much broader picture covering the entire vocalism of the Romance languages and dialects. If to this we shall add the scores for consonant changes, we shall at last have a fairly complete picture of the phonology of any language or dialect we may wish to place in the balance, with its relative degree of phonological change from the original Latin and its degree of affinity with any other language or dialect with which we may wish to compare it.

If we shall then broaden our picture by adding the sum total of significant morphological and syntactical phenomena of change, and combine our final findings with what is already known corcerning lexical proportions, we shall have achieved a fairly satisfactory description of the Romance languages and dialects in their relation to one another and to the Latin from which they sprang. We shall be able to compare them on some sort of scientific basis, and to state that there is a fundamental unity between two or more of them where such a unity really appears, discarding the hypothesis of unity where it is based solely on a few parallel developments which may be of a coincidental nature. We shall further be able to classify any language or dialect that may be under study by referring to the sum total of all its phonological, morphological, syntactical and lexical characteristics, instead of fastening upon one or two single features and proclaiming them paramount.

Since this work is still in its initial stage, the author will welcome all constructive criticism and suggestions that this article may elicit. A few such suggestions that have already reached him are the following:

1. That the comparison be between the stressed-vowel phonemic pattern of the parent-language and that of the modern descendant. While this would be an ideal method from the descriptive standpoint, it would leave out of account historical transformations; e. g., Latin ŏ > French [œ] or [ɸ], but the intervening diphthongization would be left out of the reckoning.

2. That the full measure of historical transformation, where known, be taken into account; e. g., that Latin ē or ĭ > French ei, oi, [wɛ], [wa], be counted as one diphthongization plus at least three changes (2 + 3 = 5). This would be an ideal method from the historical standpoint, but would heavily weight the scales in favor of those languages or dialects whose history is fully know, as against those which appear at a later date, with the possibility of earlier unrecorded transformations.

3. That failure to effect a normal change (Spanish *espejo*, Italian *consiglio*) be given not a minus, but a plus-value. The value of this suggestion lies especially in the fact that the regular phenomenon may have occurred, and then have been followed by a regression to the original status of the vowel by reason of the following phoneme (cf. *bŏna* > Fr. *buona* > *bone, bonne*; *hŏminem* > Sp. *huemne* > *hombre*).

4. That equal point-values be assigned to all phenomena of change, regardless of their nature; e. g., that the diphthongization of ĕ > Fr. *ie*, the transformation of *a* > *e*, and the conditioned change of *a* > *ie* after a palatal be given equal value. The statistical objection here would be that some weight should be given to those phenomena which are of constant occurrence as against those which, being conditioned upon the presence of another phoneme, are bound to occur more seldom. Also, some concession should perhaps be made to the importance of diphthongization, which some linguists consider paramount. At any rate, application of the suggested criterion combined with the preceding one gives us the following results: French, 46½%; Portuguese, 45%; Provençal, 37½%; Rumanian, 32%; Spanish, 20½%; Italian, 16%; Sardinian, 11%. While the percentages vary somewhat, the relative position of the languages does not.

5. That actual frequency of occurrence of the Latin phonemes be gauged either from a statistical study of Latin literary documents, or from a similar study of early Romance documents, so that more specific values may be assigned to each and every phoneme and its transformations. This would in itself be a gigantic task, and might not necessarily be attended by fully satisfactory results, since frequency of occurrence in literature, Latin or early Romance, may not precisely reflect frequency of ocurrence in the spoken languages.

STRESSED VOWELS (FREE) FRENCH

	Stay (0)	Diphthong-ize (2)	Change (1)	Change from Nasal (1/2)	Change from i Pal. (1/2)	Change by Umlaut (1/2)
ă			e (1)	ãi (½)	ai¹, ie² (½)	
ā			e (1)	ãi (½)	ai¹, ie² (½)	
ĕ, ae		ie (2)		iẽ (½)		
ē, oe		ei, oi (2)		ẽi, õi (½)	i³ (½)	i⁴ (¼)
ĭ		ei, oi (2)		ẽi, õi (½)		
ī	i (0)			ĩ (½)		
ŏ		uo, ue, eu (2)		õ (½)		
ō		ou, eu (2)		õ (½)		
ŭ		ou, eu (2)		õ (½)		
ū			ü (1)	ũ (½)		
au			ǫ (1)			

STRESSED VOWELS (CHECKED)

ă	a (0)			ã (½)		
ā	a (0)			ã (½)		
ĕ, ae	ę (0)			ẽ, ã (½)		
ē, oe			ę (1)	ẽ, ã (½)		i⁴ (¼)
ĭ			ę (1)	ẽ, ã (½)		
ī	i (0)			ĩ (½)		
ŏ	ǫ (0)			õ (½)		
ō			ǫ, ou⁵ (1)	õ (½)		
ŭ			ǫ, ou⁵ (1)	õ (½)		
ū			ü, ou (1)	ũ (½)		
au			ǫ (1)			

Out of a possible total of 77 change-points, French scores 34, distributed as follows: 12 from diphthongization of free vowels, 10 from modification of free and checked vowels, 10 from nasalization and other changes due to influx of following nasals, 1½ from change due to influx of palatals, ½ from umlaut. The percentage of change is over 44%.

[1] *ai* as in *factum* >*fait, pacare* > *payer*; Bourciez, § 264b.
[2] *ie* as in *canem* > *chien*; Bourciez, § 264a.
[3] *i* as in *cēra* > *cire*; Bourciez, § 264a.
[4] sporadic phenomenon, as in *fecī* > *fis, vigintī* > *vingt*, yet occurring with some regularity; only $1/_4$ point assigned; Bourciez, § 156b.
[5] not real diphthong, but only spelling to represent [u] -sound; Bourciez, § 263,c.

A NEW METHODOLOGY FOR ROMANCE CLASSIFICATIONS 131

STRESSED VOWELS (FREE) — PORTUGUESE

	Stay (0)	Diphthong-ize (2)	Change (1)	Change from Nasal (1/2)[1]	Change from Pal. (1/2)	Change by Umlaut (1/2)
ă	a (0)			ã (½)	aį > eį (½)[2]	
ā	a (0)			ã (½)	aį > eį (½)[2]	
ĕ, ae	ę (0)			ẽ (½)		ę (½)[3]
ē, oe	ę (0)			ẽ (½)		i, ę (½)[3]
ĭ			ę (1)	ẽ (½)		ę (½)[3]
ī	i (0)			ī (½)		
ŏ	ǫ (0)			õ (½)		ǫ (½)[3]
ō	ǫ (0)			õ (½)		ǫ, u (½)[3]
ŭ			ǫ (1)	õ (½)		ǫ (½)[3]
ū	u (0)			ũ (½)		
au		ou, oi (2)				

STRESSED VOWELS (CHECKED)

	Stay (0)	Diphthong-ize (2)	Change (1)	Change from Nasal (1/2)	Change from Pal. (1/2)	Change by Umlaut (1/2)
ă	a (0)			ã (½)		
ā	a (0)			ã (½)		
ĕ, ae	ę (0)			ẽ (½)		ę (½)[3]
ē, oe	ę (0)			ẽ (½)		i, ę (½)[3]
ĭ			ę (1)	ẽ (½)		ę (½)[3]
ī	i (0)			ī (½)		
ŏ	ǫ (0)			õ (½)		ǫ (½)[3]
ō	ǫ (0)			õ (½)		u, ǫ (½)[3]
ŭ			ǫ (1)	õ (½)		ǫ (½)
ū	u (0)			ũ (½)		
au		ou, oi (2)				

Out of a possible 77 change-points, Portuguese scores 25, distributed as follows: 4 from rediphthongization of *au*, 4 from modification of free or checked vowels, 10 from nasalization and other changes due to influx of nasals, 1 from change due to influx of palatals, 6 from umlaut. The percentage of change is over 31%.

[1] Williams, *From Latin to Portuguese*, § 101.
[2] as in *factum* > *feito*.
[3] Phenomena of type of *mĕtum* > *mędo*, *ista* > *ęssa*, *fŏcum* > *fǫgo*, *formōsa* > *formǫsa*, *tōtum* > *tudo*; Williams, § 100.

STRESSED VOWELS (FREE) PROVENÇAL

Stay (0)	Diphthong-ize (2)	Change (1)	Change from Nasal (1/2)	Change from Pal., Labial (1/2)	Change by Umlaut
ă	a (0)		ãi (½)		
ā	a (0)		ãi (½)		
ĕ, ae	ę (0)		ẽ, e (½)	ie (½)[1]	
ē, oe	ę (0)	ei (final; ½)[2]	ẽ, e (½)		i (¹/₄)[3]
ĭ		ei (final; ½)[2] ę (1)	ẽ, e (½)		
ī	i (0)		ĩ, i (½)		
ŏ	ǫ (0)		õ, o (½)	ue (½)[1]	
ō	ǫ (0)		õ, o (½)		
ŭ		ǫ (1)	õ, o (½)		
ū		ü (1)	ũ, u (½)		
au	au (0)				

STRESSED VOWELS (CHECKED)

ă	a (0)		ã, a (½)		
ā	a (0)		ã, a (½)		
ĕ	ę (0)		ẽ, e (½)	ie (½)[1]	
ē	ę (0)		ẽ, e (½)		i (¹/₄)[3]
ĭ		ę (½)	ẽ, e (½)		
ī	i (0)		ĩ, i (½)		
ŏ	ǫ (0)		õ, o (½)	ue (½)[1]	
ō	ǫ (0)		õ, o (½)		
ŭ		ǫ (1)	õ, o (½)		
ū		ü (1)	ũ, u (½)		
au	au (0)				

Out of a possible total of 77 change-points, Provençal scores 19½, distributed as follows: 1 from diphthongization of free vowels (only when final); 6 from other modifications in free or checked vowels; 10 from nasalization and other changes due to influx of nasals; 2 from diphthongization caused by influx of palatals or labials; ½ from umlaut phenomena. The percentage of change is over 25%.

[1] Diphthongization appears when palatal or labial follows, as in *vielh, nuech, brieu, nueu*; Bourciez, § 264c.

[2] Long *e* and short *i* diphthongize when they become final; Bourciez, § 264c.

[3] Sporadic umlaut change of *ē* to *ī*, but with some frequency; ¹/₄ point assigned; Bourciez, § 156b.

STRESSED VOWELS (FREE)					RUMANIAN
Stay (0)	Diphthong-ize (2)	Change (1)	Change from Nasal (1/2)	Change from Pal. (1/2)	Change by Umlaut (1/2)
ă	a (0)		î (½)¹		
ā	a (0)		î (½)¹		
ĕ, ae		ie (2)	i (½)¹		ia (½)²
ē, oe	ę (0)		i (½)¹		ea (½)²
ĭ		ę (1)			ea (½)²
ī	i (0)				
ŏ	ǫ (0)		u (½)¹		oa (½)²
ō	ǫ (0)		u (½)¹		oa (½)²
ŭ	u (0)				oa (½)²
ū	u (0)				
au	au (0)				
STRESSED VOWELS (CHECKED)					
ă	a (0)		î (½)¹		
ā	a (0)		î (½)¹		
ĕ, ae		ie (2)	i (½)¹		ia (½)²
ē, oe	ę (0)		i (½)¹		ea (½)²
ĭ		ę (1)	i (½)¹		ea (½)²
ī	i (0)				
ŏ	ǫ (0)		u (½)¹		oa (½)²
ō	ǫ (0)		u (½)¹		oa (½)²
ŭ	u (0)				
ū	u (0)				
au	au (0)				

Out of a possible total of 77 change-points, Rumanian scores 18, distributed as follows: 4 from diphthongization of free or checked vowels, 2 from modification of free or checked vowels; 6½ from changes due to influx of a nasal; 5½ from umlaut. The percentage of change is 23½%.

[1] Phenomena of the type of *lana* > *lînă*, *campum* > *cîmp*, *bŏnum* > *bun*, *běne* > *bine*, etc.; Bourciez, § 459.

[2] Phenomena of the type of *pĕtra* > *piatră*, *dirēcta* > *dreaptă*, *sōlem* > *soare*, *pŏrta* > *poartă*, etc.; Bourciez, § 459.

STRESSED VOWELS (FREE) — SPANISH

Stay (0)	Diphthong-ize (2)	Change (1)	Change from Pal., Hiatus, etc. (1/2)	No change from Pal. (— 1/2)	Change by Umlaut (1/2)
ă	a (0)		a̦i > e (½)[1]		
ā	a (0)		a̦i > e (½)[1]		
ĕ, ae		ie (2)	i (½)[1]		
ē, oe	ę (0)				i (¼)[2]
ĭ		ę (1)			
ī	i (0)				
ŏ		ue (2)			
ō	ǫ (0)				
ŭ		ǫ (1)			
ū	u (0)				
au		ǫ (1)			

STRESSED VOWELS (CHECKED)

ă	a (0)				
ā	a (0)				
ĕ, ae		ie (2)	i (½)[1]	e (—½)[3]	
ē, oe	ę (0)				i (¼)[2]
ĭ		ę (1)			
ī	i (0)				
ŏ		ue (2)		o (—½)[3]	
ō	ǫ (0)				
ŭ		ǫ (1)			
ū	u (0)				
au		ǫ (1)			

Out of a possible total of 77 change-points, Spanish scores 15½, distributed as follows: 8 from diphthongization of free or checked vowels; 6 from modification of free or checked vowels; 2 from changes due to influx of following palatal (i); ½ from umlaut; —1 from failure to undergo normal change because of following palatal. The percentage of change is 20%.

[1] Phenomena of the type of *leche, pido, sirvo, silla, mio*; Meyer-Lübke, *Grammaire des langues romanes*, § 156.

[2] Sporadic phenomenon, as in *fecī > hice, sepia > jibia*, yet occurring with some frequency; $1/4$ point assigned; Bourciez, § 156, b, c.

[3] Lack of normal diphthongization caused by following palatal, as in *spĕculum > espejo, nŏctem > noche*; Bourciez, § 154d.

STRESSED VOWELS (FREE) — ITALIAN

Stay (0)	Diphthong-ize (2)	Change (1)	Change from i Pal., Hiatus (1/2)	No Change from i Pal., Nasal, Hiatus (— 1/2)
ă	a (0)			
ā	a (0)			
ĕ, ae		ie (2)	i (½)[1]	
ē, oe	ę (0)			
ĭ		ę (1)		i (—½)[2]
ī	i (0)			
ŏ		uo (2)	u (½)[1]	
ō	ǫ (0)			
ŭ		ǫ (1)		u (—½)[2]
ū	u (0)			
au		ǫ (1)		

STRESSED VOWELS (CHECKED)

ă	a (0)			
ā	a (0)			
ĕ, ae	ę (0)			
ē, oe	ę (0)			
ĭ		ę (1)		i (—½)[2]
ī	i (0)			
ŏ	ǫ (0)			
ō	ǫ (0)			
ŭ		ǫ (1)		u (—½)[2]
ū	u (0)			
au		ǫ (1)		

Out of a possible 77 change-points, Italian scores 9, distributed as follows: 4 from diphthongization of free vowels; 6 from modification of free or checked vowels; 1 from changes due to influx of following i̯, palatal or hiatus, —2 from lack of normal change due to influx of following nasal liquid or hiatus. The percentage of change is 12%.

[1] Phenomena of the type of *Dĕum* > *Dio, ego* > *io, bŏvem* > *bue*; Pei, *Italian Language*, § 48.

[2] Conservation of *i, u* in *consiglio, pugno, via, tuo*, etc.; Pei, § 48.

	Stay (0)	Diphthong-ize (2)	Change (1)	Change from Pal., Nasal (1/2)	SARDINIAN Change by Umlaut (1/2)
STRESSED VOWELS (FREE)					
ă	a (0)				
ā	a (0)				
ĕ, ae	ę (0)				ę (½)[1]
ē, oe	ę (0)				ę (½)[1]
ĭ	i (0)				
ī	i (0)				
ŏ	ǫ (0)				ǫ (½)[1]
ō	ǫ (0)				ǫ (½)[1]
ŭ	u (0)				
ū	u (0)				
au			a (1)[2]		
STRESSED VOWELS (CHECKED)					
ă	a (0)				
ā	a (0)				
ĕ, ae	ę (0)				ę (½)[1]
ē, oe	ę (0)				ę (½)[1]
ĭ	i (0)				
ī	i (0)				
ŏ	ǫ (0)				ǫ (½)[1]
ō	ǫ (0)				ǫ (½)[1]
ŭ	u (0)				
ū	u (0)				
au			a (1)[2]		

Out of a possible total of 77 change-points, Sardinian scores 6, distributed as follows: 2 from change of *au* to *a*; 4 from umlaut changes. The percentage of change is 8%.

[1] *Sŏmnum* > *sǫmnu*, *cōnca* > *cǫnca*, etc.; Meyer-Lübke, § 129.
[2] *Causa* > *casa*, *laurum* > *laru*; Bourciez, § 160.

Word, V (1949)

www.ingramcontent.com/pod-product-compliance
Lightning Source LLC
Chambersburg PA
CBHW021846220426
43663CB00005B/426